CONTENTS

STATEMENTS OF COMMITTEE MEMBERS

Brownback, Hon. Sam, a U.S. Senator from the State of Kansas 7
Cantwell, Hon. Maria, a U.S. Senator from the State of Washington 9
DeWine, Hon. Mike, a U.S. Senator from the State of Ohio 72
Grassley, Hon. Charles E., a U.S. Senator from the State of Iowa 75
Kennedy, Hon. Edward M., a U.S. Senator from the State of Massachusetts ... 1

WITNESSES

Butterfield, Jeanne A., Executive Director, American Immigration Lawyers Association, Washington, D.C. 41
Gutierrez, Lino, Acting Assistant Secretary of State for Western Hemisphere Affairs, Department of State, Washington, D.C. 19
Norton, Richard E., Executive Director, International Biometric Industry Association, Fairfax, Virginia 64
Papademitriou, Demetrios G., Co-Director, Migration Policy Institute, Washington, D.C. 53
Ryan, Mary A., Assistant Secretary of State for Consular Affairs, Department of State, Washington, D.C. 11
Ziglar, James W., Commissioner, Immigration and Naturalization Service, Department of Justice, Washington, D.C. 24

S. Hrg. 107–651

EFFECTIVE IMMIGRATION CONTROLS TO DETER TERRORISM

HEARING

BEFORE THE

SUBCOMMITTEE ON IMMIGRATION

OF THE

COMMITTEE ON THE JUDICIARY

UNITED STATES SENATE

ONE HUNDRED SEVENTH CONGRESS

FIRST SESSION

OCTOBER 17, 2001

Serial No. J–107–45

Printed for the use of the Committee on the Judiciary

U.S. GOVERNMENT PRINTING OFFICE

81–651 PDF WASHINGTON : 2002

For sale by the Superintendent of Documents, U.S. Government Printing Office
Internet: bookstore.gpo.gov Phone: toll free (866) 512–1800; DC area (202) 512–1800
Fax: (202) 512–2250 Mail: Stop SSOP, Washington, DC 20402–0001

COMMITTEE ON THE JUDICIARY

PATRICK J. LEAHY, Vermont, *Chairman*

EDWARD M. KENNEDY, Massachusetts	ORRIN G. HATCH, Utah
JOSEPH R. BIDEN, JR., Delaware	STROM THURMOND, South Carolina
HERBERT KOHL, Wisconsin	CHARLES E. GRASSLEY, Iowa
DIANNE FEINSTEIN, California	ARLEN SPECTER, Pennsylvania
RUSSELL D. FEINGOLD, Wisconsin	JON KYL, Arizona
CHARLES E. SCHUMER, New York	MIKE DEWINE, Ohio
RICHARD J. DURBIN, Illinois	JEFF SESSIONS, Alabama
MARIA CANTWELL, Washington	SAM BROWNBACK, Kansas
JOHN EDWARDS, North Carolina	MITCH MCCONNELL, Kentucky

BRUCE A. COHEN, *Majority Chief Counsel and Staff Director*
SHARON PROST, *Minority Chief Counsel*
MAKAN DELRAHIM, *Minority Staff Director*

SUBCOMMITTEE ON IMMIGRATION

EDWARD M. KENNEDY, Massachusetts, *Chairman*

DIANNE FEINSTEIN, California	SAM BROWNBACK, Kansas
CHARLES E. SCHUMER, New York	ARLEN SPECTER, Pennsylvania
RICHARD J. DURBIN, Illinois	CHARLES E. GRASSLEY, Iowa
MARIA CANTWELL, Washington	JON KYL, Arizona
JOHN EDWARDS, North Carolina	MIKE DEWINE, Ohio

MELODY BARNES, *Majority Chief Counsel*
STUART ANDERSON, *Minority Chief Counsel*

EFFECTIVE IMMIGRATION CONTROLS TO DETER TERRORISM

WEDNESDAY, OCTOBER 17, 2001

UNITED STATES SENATE,
SUBCOMMITTEE ON IMMIGRATION,
COMMITTEE ON THE JUDICIARY,
Washington, D.C.

The Subcommittee met, pursuant to notice, at 10:36 a.m., in Room SD–226, Dirksen Senate Office Building, Hon. Edward M. Kennedy, Chairman of the Subcommittee, presiding.

Present: Senators Kennedy, Cantwell, Brownback, Grassley, and DeWine.

OPENING STATEMENT OF HON. EDWARD M. KENNEDY, A U.S. SENATOR FROM THE STATE OF MASSACHUSETTS

Chairman KENNEDY. We will come to order. We know that there has been some news affecting exposures to anthrax to some of the staff in our buildings and that is being dealt with very effectively by the Sergeant at Arms and by the health professionals that have been assigned to deal with that job. We feel strongly, since immigration issues have important implications in terms of national security and also to terrorism, that it was important that we move ahead.

We have legislation that Senator Brownback and I have been working on which we intend to introduce shortly. We have been getting some good suggestions and recommendations from the administration and from other groups. But we are very strongly committed to moving in this area. There are many aspects we must address. There are our combat troops, there is money laundering, and also the development of effective bioterrorist abilities. We are dealing as well with the challenges of immigration as well as the challenges in the intelligence community. So all of these make up very important aspects in dealing with terrorism. It was our judgment that we ought to move ahead with this hearing, and we are very grateful to all of our witnesses here this morning.

It is a privilege to chair this hearing today on the critical issue of border security and its critical importance in preventing terrorism. And I welcome all our distinguished witnesses and commend them for their commitment to this important issue. I look forward to hearing from them today and working with my colleagues to protect our borders effectively and fairly.

Strengthening the security of our borders is an indispensable part of this Nation's effort to prevent future terrorist attacks. We must develop policies and enact laws that meet the serious security threats we face from abroad, and we must do so without obstructing the entry of the more than 31 million foreign nationals who legally enter the United States each year.

Clearly, the screening of foreign nationals who seek entry into the United States must be improved. To do so, we must make better use of intelligence information to identify high-risk individuals who are potential terrorists and make sure that the information is in the hands of the proper authorities in time to act.

Accurate and timely intelligence is critical. Federal intelligence and law enforcement agencies maintain lookout lists containing the names of foreign nationals who pose a threat to our safety and security. To keep these persons out of the United States, intelligence agencies and law enforcement agencies must be able to share and update this critical information with the Department of State and the Immigration and Naturalization Service as quickly as possible.

The Office of Homeland Security should coordinate the implementation of a comprehensive data-sharing system to provide these front-line agencies with the critical information that they need.

Weaknesses exist in the lookout system. Potential terrorists often use aliases and obtain false or stolen identification. Biometric identification technology can be used to improve the reliability of the lookout lists and enhance border security. Their use should be significantly expanded, for inclusion in passports, visas, and other travel papers.

Biometric technology should also be used to screen incoming travelers. Automated systems, such as INSPASS, should be expanded where practical to screen low-risk travelers.

The United States, Canada, and Mexico can clearly do more to coordinate border efforts against terrorists. Efforts to share lookout lists, develop and improve joint inspection regimes and facilities, and train intelligence and other enforcement personnel should be expanded.

Yesterday, Senator Brownback and I met with our two Ambassadors from Canada and Mexico who made good recommendations, and today earlier we met with the Deputy Prime Minister of Canada, who also had useful suggestions.

In addition, we should work more closely with our European allies and other countries to develop agreements to share intelligence databases and collect information on persons who have engaged in terrorist activity or who may be a threat. And up until the law which has just passed the Senate, there was a prohibition of sharing that information, both for the United States and also in gaining that information. We have made progress on that in the legislation which is pending action now in the conference.

We should also expand the number of pre-clearance sites abroad. Currently, most foreign nationals are inspected by immigration officers upon arrival at U.S. ports of entry. Use of pre-clearance sites allows more time for thorough inspections and can lead to the apprehension of suspected terrorists before they arrive in the U.S.

Many airlines transmit their passenger lists to the destination airports, enabling U.S. authorities to investigate the list while the planes are en route. Transmittal of these lists is currently being used in 75 to 80 percent of all cases, but it should be used for all international flights.

In addition, full implementation of an automated exit/entry system will enable the INS to monitor foreign nationals in the U.S. more effectively. Implementation of this system has been delayed because the INS has lacked the technology to implement this measure at all ports of entry, especially at the land borders.

I know Mr. Ziglar has made this case appearing before other Committees about the importance of getting the resources. We support those requests, and they should be given a high priority.

Federal funding is also needed to implement and effectively operate the electronic foreign student tracking system enacted in 1996.

A related issue is the large number of U.S. educational institutions authorized to enroll foreign students. Periodic review is needed to ensure that these institutions are professional and competent. That hasn't been done in the past. It will be done in the future.

The implementation of all these tracking systems will enable the INS to determine whether foreign nationals have complied with the terms of their visas and help to enhance our security and safety by identifying possible threats. We can protect our Nation's security, without undermining our history and heritage as a Nation of immigrants.

[The prepared statement and an attachment of Senator Kennedy follow.]

STATEMENT OF HON. EDWARD M. KENNEDY, A U.S. SENATOR FROM THE STATE OF MASSACHUSETTS

It's a privilege to chair this hearing today on the critical issue of border security and its critical importance in preventing terrorism. I welcome all our distinguished witnesses and I commend them for their commitment to this important issue. I look forward to hearing from them today and to working with my colleagues to protect our borders effectively and fairly.

Strengthening the security of our borders is an indispensable part of the nation's effort to prevent future terrorist attacks. We must develop policies and enact laws that meet the serious security threats we face from abroad, and we must do so without obstructing the entry of the more than 31 million foreign nationals who legally enter the United States each year.

Clearly, the screening of foreign nationals who seek entry into the U.S. must be improved. To do so, we must make better use of intelligence information to identify high risk individuals who are potential terrorists, and make sure that the information is in the hands of the proper authorities in time to act.

Accurate and timely intelligence is critical. Federal intelligence and law enforcement agencies maintain "lookout lists" containing the names of foreign nationals who pose a threat to our safety and security. To keep these persons out of the United States, intelligence agencies and law enforcement agencies must be able to share and update this critical information with the Department of State and the Immigration and Naturalization Service as quickly as possible.

The Office of Homeland Security should coordinate the implementation of a comprehensive data sharing system to provide these front line agencies with the critical information they need.

Weaknesses exist in the lookout systems. Potential terrorists often use aliases and obtain false or stolen identification. Biometric identification technology can be used to improve the reliability of the lookout lists and enhance border security. Their use should be significantly expanded, for inclusion in passports, visas and other travel papers.

Biometric technology should also be used to screen incoming travelers. Automated systems, such as INPASS, should be expanded where practicable to screen low-risk travelers.

The United States, Canada, and Mexico can clearly do more to coordinate border efforts against terrorists. Efforts to share lookout lists, develop and improve joint inspection regimes and facilities, and train intelligence and other enforcement personnel should be expanded.

In addition, we should work more closely with our European allies and other countries to develop agreements to share intelligence databases and collect information on persons who have engaged in terrorist activity or who may be a threat.

We should also expand the number of pre-clearance sites abroad. Currently, most foreign nationals are inspected by immigration officers upon arrival at U.S. ports of entry. Use of pre-clearance sites allows more time for thorough inspections, and can lead to the apprehension of suspected terrorists before they arrive in the U. S.

Many airlines transmit their passenger lists to the destination airports, enabling U.S. authorities to investigate the list while the planes are en route. Transmittal of these lists is currently being used in 75–80% of all cases, but it should be used for all international flights.

In addition, full implementation of an automated exit/entry system will enable the INS to monitor foreign nationals in the U.S. more effectively. Implementation of this system has been delayed because the INS has lacked the technology to implement this measure at all ports of entry, especially at the land borders.

Federal funding is also needed to implement and effectively operate the electronic foreign student tracking system enacted in 1996.

A related issue is the large number of U.S. educational institutions authorized to enroll foreign students. Periodic review is needed to ensure that these institutions are professional and competent.

The implementation of all of these tracking systems will enable the INS to determine whether foreign nationals have complied with the terms of their visas, and help to enhance our safety and security by identifying possible threats. We can protect our nation's security, without undermining our history and heritage as a nation of immigrants.

Again I thank the witnesses for being here, and I look forward to their testimony.

EFFECTIVE IMMIGRATION CONTROLS TO DETER TERRORISM

OCTOBER 17, 2001

The terrorist attacks on September 11 made clear that the United States current intelligence and terrorism prevention net leaves us vulnerable to serious security dangers. Strengthening immigration laws should be an indispensable part of the nation's efforts to prevent future terrorist attacks. Effective immigration and border controls can have a significant impact on our national security.

This week, Senator Edward M. Kennedy, joined by Senator Sam Brownback (R–KS), is introducing legislation that will institute new procedures and dedicate new resources to increase the likelihood that potential terrorists can be detected and apprehended before they act. This legislation will significantly improve the screening of foreign nationals seeking entry into the U.S. and better secure the nation's borders. By making better use of intelligence information to identify high risk individuals who seek to harm us, and ensuring that timely information is in the hands of the proper authorities, this legislation will help the nation meet the serious security threats we face from abroad, without obstructing the free flow of goods across our borders or the entry of the more than 31 million foreign nationals who legally enter the U.S. each year as visitors, students, and temporary workers.

This legislation will increase the development and implementation of effective immigration controls to deter terrorism.

INTELLIGENCE. TECHNOLOGY, AND COOPERATION

Accurate and Timely Intelligence Is Critical

Federal intelligence and law enforcement agencies maintain "lookout lists" containing the names of foreign nationals who should not be admitted to the U.S. These are individuals who have criminal records, who have been denied visas or previously deported, who are suspected terrorists, or who require serious scrutiny for other reasons. To successfully prevent the admission of these persons into the U.S., all intelligence agencies and law enforcement agencies, including the CIA, DIA, NSA, and FBI, must share this critical information with the Department of State and the Immigration and Naturalization Service in a timely manner.

Currently, some of this information is not shared with these two agencies, which are responsible for making determinations about who is granted a visa or is admitted to the U.S. Legislation is now pending which will provide the Department of State and INS with electronic access to the FBI's criminal history databases. The Department of State and the INS should also have electronic access to all lookout lists maintained by the CIA, DIA, NSA and FBI. The new Office of Homeland Security should coordinate the implementation of a comprehensive data sharing system to provide these front line agencies with the critical information they need Senator Kennedy's legislation will require the prompt development and implementation of a plan to provide the State Department and the INS with timely electronic access to all lookout lists maintained by the CIA, DIA, NSA and FBI.

Biometric Technology Can Improve Security

Weaknesses exist in the lookout systems in terms of identifying terrorists seeking visas. Potential terrorists often use aliases and obtain false or stolen identification. Biometric identification technology can improve the reliability of the lookout lists and enhance border security. The most common biometric data include fingerprint and hand imaging, iris and retina scans, and facial recognition. These data cannot be borrowed, or stolen, and forging them is extremely difficult. These new technologies can match a unique identifying characteristic of an individual with a name, and they need to be used effectively.

Machine-readable passports and visas are becoming more prevalent and more difficult to counterfeit. Biometric data are currently being incorporated into some immigration documents, and their use should be significantly expanded, for inclusion in passports, visas and other travel documents. With such technology, a traveler's identity can be quickly and definitively verified by matching the identity with biometric data incorporated in their documents.

Biometric technology should also be used to screen incoming travelers. Systems, such as INPASS, which use biometric imaging, have proven successful in screening frequent low-risk travelers. Such systems should be expanded where practicable, since they enable more resources to be allocated to anti-terrorist and security activities.

This legislation will authorize funding to study, develop and implement the use of biometric identifiers in passports, visas and other immigration documents, and the use of biometric technologies to screen incoming travelers to the U.S.

A North American System

The U.S., Canada, and Mexico can clearly do more to coordinate border efforts against terrorists. Cooperation between our countries can be strengthened, taking into account each other's security concerns, while still facilitating the movement of goods and persons. Efforts to share lookout lists, develop and improve joint inspection regimes and facilities, and train intelligence and other enforcement personnel should be expanded.

Criminal smuggling rings, with knowledge of the weaknesses in our border security, have developed into multi-billion-dollar-a-year operations, and potential terrorists could use these smuggling operations to cross the border. Detecting and shutting down smuggling operations requires close cross-border cooperation, and these border security efforts must be strengthened.

In addition, we should work more closely with our European allies and other countries, to develop reciprocal agreements to share intelligence databases and collect information on persons who may be a potential threat or who have engaged in terrorist activity.

This legislation authorizes the Department of State and INS, in conjunction with the Office of Homeland Security, to study the costs, procedures and implementation of a Perimeter National Security Program for the U.S., Canada, and Mexico. It will also authorize a substantial increase in staffing and resources for the INS and Department of State to enhance security along the nation's borders.

SCREENING INDIVIDUALS BEFORE THEY ARRIVE IN THE U.S.

Consular Offices: The First Line of Defense

Most foreign nationals traveling to the United States must apply for visas from U.S. consulates abroad. Consular officers, who tend to be junior personnel with little job experience, interview applicants to determine whether they are eligible for visas. Until now, consular screening has focused primarily on detecting visa overstayers, examining indicators such as bank accounts, which have no bearing on whether the applicant is a security risk. Although this focus is important, more emphasis is needed on issues of security. We should build a corps of knowledgeable and experienced consular officers, skilled in screening for security threats.

This legislation will require the Department of State to provide specialized training for consular officers in the effective screening of visa applicants who pose a potential threat to the U.S.

Immigration Checks at Airports Abroad:

Foreign nationals are generally inspected by immigration officers upon arrival at U.S. ports of entry. In some high-volume airports abroad, U.S. immigration checks are performed at pre-clearance sites at the point of departure, where travel documents are inspected before an individual boards a U.S.-bound plane. Pre-clearance sites should be expanded. They allow more time for thorough inspection. While a U.S. inspector has no authority to arrest a suspected terrorist at a pre-clearance site, the U.S. could cooperate with authorities who do have the power to apprehend suspects.

This legislation will examine the expansion of pre-flight inspection sites abroad, including the number, location, cost, staffing, and training of personnel.

Sharing Passenger Lists:

Once travelers have boarded, many airlines voluntarily transmit the passenger manifest to the destination airports. Passenger lists are investigated while the planes are enroute. Once the planes have landed, authorities can intercept passengers who are on the lookout lists. Transmittal of airline manifests is currently being used in 75–80% of all cases, but it should be used for all international flights. The State Department should also transmit electronic versions of its visa files to inspectors, so they are available at the time of inspection.

This legislation will require all international commercial air carriers to provide passenger manifest information in advance of arrival.

MONITORING FOREIGN NATIONALS IN THE U.S.

Automated Exit/Entry System

Upon arriving in the U.S., non-citizens, including permanent residents and temporary foreign visitors, workers, and students, complete a form, called the I–94 form, which they are supposed to return when they leave the country. Upon departure, travelers are required to return the I–94 forms to airline representatives, who are supposed to turn them over to the INS. Compliance is inconsistent, as not all carriers return the I–94 forms to the INS.

Persons leaving the country at land borders are also supposed to turn in I-94 forms, but many do not. These forms are currently completed by hand, and cannot be used to track the departure of specific persons until entered into a computer.

In 1996, Congress enacted legislation mandating the development of an automated entry/exit control system to record the entry of every non-citizen arriving in the U.S. and match it with a record of departure. The INS lacked the technology to implement this needed measure at all ports of entry, especially at the land borders, without serious disruptions. Last year, Congress enacted legislation to establish reasonable implementation deadlines. The Attorney General is required to implement the integrated system by December 31, 2003 at all air and sea ports. For the 50 busiest land border ports of entry, the system would be implemented by December 31, 2004, and for all other land border ports, by December 31, 2005.

Technology is available to implement electronic entry/exit controls at all air and sea ports, but it is costly. Other countries utilize electronic controls that could be models for a similar U.S. program. For example, Australia has an electronic visa that is incorporated into the airline ticket. Implementation should be funded by the federal government, and airline compliance should be mandatory.

Since implementation at land borders is more difficult and has the potential of disrupting commerce, additional time and resources will be needed to establish effective exit controls at these borders. In the meantime, other steps can be taken. The U.S. has experimented with commuter lanes that permit officials to pre-screen applicants, and to issue more secure documentation and devices for automobiles, to expedite crossings without sacrificing security. Such programs should be expanded to permit rapid crossings of low-risk commuters and enable the INS to concentrate its resources on those who have not been pre-screened.

This legislation will authorize funding to implement an automated entry/exit system at all ports of entry, using technology standards, biometric identifiers, and machine readable documents to confirm and record identity. It will also expand the use of existing automated systems at land ports of entry to screen low-risk travelers.

Monitoring Foreign Students. In 1996, Congress established a program to collect information on non-immigrant foreign students and exchange program participants. The CIPRIS program was designed to apply to non-immigrants with F (student), J (exchange visitor), or M (vocational) visas. Information collected includes name and current address, major field of study, termination date and reason for termination, the number of credits completed per year, and any disciplinary action taken against the student.

A pilot phase of this program ended in 1999, but the system has not been implemented nationwide. Universities and colleges expressed serious concerns about the costs and administrative burdens of the tracking program. Some of these concerns were addressed in legislation last year, but other problems persist. They include lack of adequate funding for State Department consular operations and INS monitoring systems; gaps in reporting systems that make it impossible for the INS to know when foreign students leave, or when they fail to show up for their programs; and inadequate support for university officials responsible for ensuring compliance with visa requirements.

Federal funding is critical to implement and effectively operate the this tracking system. The INS has estimated that the cost of implementation is approximately $32 million over the next three years. Gaps in the tracking program should be closed by requiring the INS to notify institutions of a student's entry into the U.S., and requiring institutions to report to the INS the non-appearance of any student reported and any student who heaves the program.

A related problem is the large number of U.S. educational institutions authorized to issue forms to allow foreign students to obtain visas. Currently, more than 26,000 institutions are authorized to enroll foreign students. Periodic review is warranted to ensure that these institutions are professional and competent. They should certify that they agree to comply with the reporting and recordkeeping responsibilities or risk losing their authority to enroll foreign students.

This legislation will authorize funding to implement the automated student tracking system, expand the types of schools covered by the system to into include flight, language, and other vocational schools, close gaps in record keeping and reporting requirements, and require a review of institutions authorized to enroll foreign students.

An Integrated Approach

The implementation of an automated entry/exit system and the student tracking system will notify authorities whether foreign nationals have left the country under the terms of their visas, and whether foreign students are properly maintaining their status.

But, it is important to remember that foreign students represent less than two percent of the 30 million temporary visitors admitted annually to the U.S. And the vast majority of foreign visitors, students and workers who may overstay their visas are not criminals or terrorists.

Focusing INS resources on those who fail to comply with the terms of their visas will do little to enhance our national security. Linking these tracking systems to lookout systems and law enforcement databases, however, will enable the INS and law enforcement agencies to screen foreign nationals more closely and identify and apprehend those who do present a threat to our national security.

This legislation will authorize the development of a cross-agency, cost-effective electronic system to enable tracking systems to be interfaced with intelligence and law enforcement data systems.

Again, I want to thank our witnesses for being here, and I will recognize Senator Brownback for his comments.

STATEMENT OF HON. SAM BROWNBACK, A U.S. SENATOR FROM THE STATE OF KANSAS

Senator BROWNBACK. Thank you very much, Mr. Chairman. I appreciate that and I appreciate our witnesses, and I think this is a most timely and pressing topic in our combating terrorism and our protection of our people and our way of life.

First, let me applaud the efforts of this Congress to react promptly to the terrorist threats that face us. In only a month's time, our represented officials came together and passed an extensive anti-terrorist package, a tough, thoughtful, bipartisan piece of legislation, along with a number of other pieces of legislation, to allow us, to help us to combat this war on terrorism. That will arm our Government well in the fight against terrorism.

I also applaud several of our colleagues, Senators Feinstein and Kyl, for their insightful hearing last week on technology and terrorism and this Subcommittee for today's hearing on effective immigration controls to deter terrorism. Personally, I find the commitment and patriotism that echoes through these halls to be truly inspirational. United we do stand.

Nonetheless, the terrorist attacks of September 11th have unsettled the public's confidence in our Nation's security and have raised questions about whether our institutions are up to the task of intercepting and thwarting would-be terrorists. Given that the persons responsible for the attacks on the World Trade Center and the Pentagon came from overseas, our citizens understandably ask how these people entered the United States and what can be done to prevent their kind from doing so again.

Clearly, our immigration laws and policies are instrumental to the war on terrorism. While the battle may be waged on many fronts, for the man and woman on the streets immigration is the front line.

Of course, we must be vigilant not to punish the innocent in our efforts to ferret out the criminal, nor should we allow our values or out economy to be compromised. But we have a duty to the American people to take measured steps to keep terrorists from reaching our shores.

At this stage we must get a clear lay of the land. We must assess precisely where our immigration laws and practices are succeeding and where they must be improved.

The war against terrorism is a war won by information. The more information we have, the better our chances of winning. The more information our defenders can share, the stronger our line of defenses. The better grasp we have on our immigration procedures and practices, the better we can secure our borders and our safety.

Mr. Chairman, I am hopeful that this hearing will bring to light how best to utilize our immigration laws and resources to deter terrorism. I look forward to hearing the insights and recommendations of our officials from the Immigration and Naturalization Service and from the Department of State. I welcome the testimony of our learned witnesses from the public sector.

I might add my comments as well to the comments that Senator Kennedy put forward about we are working together on a bipartisan piece of legislation to try to address specific areas where there may be difficulties, where we need to tighten up overall on our immigration system. People in this country deserve a system that allows people into the country that want to be helpful to America, but keeps people from the country who want to harm this country. And I think that is all of our goals and our objectives. And we have put forward, as Senator Kennedy has articulated, several ideas already that we think would be useful in pressing this forward to secure our borders in the front-line war, and that front line in this war on terrorism being the immigration policies and procedures that we practice as a country. I look forward to your comments.

Chairman KENNEDY. Thank you very much.

Senator Cantwell has been very much involved in the development of our legislation on immigration policy issues, and we welcome her, if she would say a word.

STATEMENT OF HON. MARIA CANTWELL, A U.S. SENATOR FROM THE STATE OF WASHINGTON

Senator CANTWELL. Thank you, Mr. Chairman. I thank Senator Kennedy for holding this hearing on what I consider to be one of the most important issues in the fight against terrorism. How can we effectively secure our borders from terrorists? By improving the quality and sharing of identity information; improving the screening of foreign nationals seeking entry on U.S. visas; improving the awareness of comings and goings of these foreign nationals as they enter and exit our country; and increasing the number of Border Patrol and immigration personnel at our borders.

Mr. Chairman, we must strengthen the security at our border. Last week, we passed a major anti-terrorism bill that contained a number of provisions that will enable law enforcement and the community of intelligence gatherers to obtain and share vital information regarding persons who are a threat to the U.S.

One of the most important new tools I was pleased to have included in this legislation is the requirement that State and Justice develop a visa technology standard based on biometrics to help secure our border and make certain each individual who seeks entry into our country on a visa is the person he or she claims to be and that there is no reason to keep that person out of the country.

American citizens and the citizenship that they get comes with a deeply valued privilege, and that is the right to privacy. But to require a fingerprint or digital photograph of an alien seeking to enter our country is a reasonable and effective way to improve our ability to keep terrorists out of the country while still welcoming a vibrant flow of legal aliens.

Aliens seeking to visit, to go to school, work, engage in business will provide the consular office considering that visa application with some type of biometrics, most likely fingerprint and digital photograph, so that we can compare the identity information with that of persons who are unwelcome in the United States. With this technology, we will be able to confirm the person presenting a visa at the border with the information that they need.

The technology standard is not prescriptive, and I am well aware that there are many different types of technologies available here and in Canada and in other places. And I have left it to the agencies to determine what type of information sharing should be required as part of the visa program.

Let me note that I recognize that technology will be only as good as the information system which it is put into, and, therefore, facilitating a technology that compels cooperation between agencies will be very important. I hope to aid in changing the non-technology barriers to data sharing.

Further, I am willing to work with the chairman and Senator Brownback and my other colleagues to assure that uniform practices that will feed the system with critical information on the State Department and INS need to be also working on an international basis with our allies so that our northern perimeter will be as good as that technology standard.

Mr. Chairman, again, I look forward to hearing the comments from the witness, and thank you for holding this very important meeting.

Chairman KENNEDY. Thank you.

We have been joined by Senator Grassley.

Senator GRASSLEY. Thank you very much, Mr. Chairman.

I think that we need to better share information. The INS needs all relevant information at its disposal that will identify and track down immigrants who are on watch lists of other countries.

The second point I would make is that we should implement technologies needed to prevent illegal or criminal aliens from entering. We need to create tamper-resistant visas and passports. We need to invest in an effective biometric system and provide the scanners to read the information on border crossing cards. I know that Mr. Ziglar is going to lay out about that testimony and has instructed his staff to expedite database improvements. He specifically mentions the Student Exchange Visitor Information System.

Unfortunately, delay in the implementation of this system has and may continue to have detrimental effects on our Nation's security, and that is very unacceptable. We want to help the colleges and universities, and in turn, I believe that colleges will want to help us in our war on terrorism.

Pursuant to this, I wrote Attorney General John Ashcroft and requested immediate consideration of Federal funding to speed up implementation of the student tracking system. I propose that the Justice Department use a portion of the emergency anti-terrorism funds approved by Congress to fund the start-up of the student tracking system. Additionally, the Department should clearly outline the responsibilities of schools who wish to retain foreign students.

Finally, I realize that the Immigration Service does not have the enforcement tools to go after every foreign student whose visa expires. And even if Federal agencies are sharing data and using the best technology we can create, the INS will still face problems in catching the bad guys.

These are situations in which we can enlist State and local support. By implementing Section 133 of the Illegal Immigration Reform and Immigrant Responsibility Act, the Department of Justice can enter into agreements with local law enforcement agencies in order to allow qualified officers to help in the investigation, apprehension, and detention of illegal aliens.

The enemy could be among us, and the threat certainly remains before us. Now is the time to act on what we know are problems. I already identified a number of problems and concrete solutions. We need to move forward with the proposals that we have discussed since September the 11th.

I thank you, Chairman Kennedy.

Chairman KENNEDY. Thank you very much.

It is an honor to introduce our first panel: Assistant Secretary of State Mary Ryan; Acting Assistant Secretary Lino Gutierrez; and INS Commissioner James Ziglar.

Ambassador Ryan has been a distinguished leader at the State Department since she joined the Foreign Service in 1966. She became Assistant Secretary of State for Consular Affairs in 1993. Before that, she had served as Deputy Assistant Secretary in the Bureau of European and Canadian Affairs, as Ambassador to Swaziland, and in numerous embassies and positions in the State Department.

Ambassador Gutierrez has also had a distinguished career in the State Department, where he is now Acting Assistant Secretary for Western Hemisphere Affairs. He has served as Ambassador to Nicaragua and has also been posted to the Dominican Republic, Portugal, France, and the Bahamas, and has extensive knowledge on border security issues.

Commissioner Ziglar is well respected by all of us in the Senate who know him well, and I am honored to welcome him back to this Committee in his new position as the Commissioner of Immigration and Naturalization Service. Mr. Ziglar worked closely with all of us in the Senate in his outstanding years as the Senate Sergeant-at–Arms. He has also served as a managing director of Paine Webber and Drexel Burnham Lambert, as Assistant Secretary of the Interior for Water and Science. He had also practiced law for many years and was a clerk on the U.S. Supreme Court for Justice Harry Blackmun.

I thank all of you for being here. We will recognize Ms. Ryan.

STATEMENT OF MARY A. RYAN, ASSISTANT SECRETARY OF STATE FOR CONSULAR AFFAIRS, DEPARTMENT OF STATE, WASHINGTON, D.C.

Ms. RYAN. Mr. Chairman, members of the Committee, thank you for the opportunity to appear before you today to explain the role of the Bureau of Consular Affairs, and most particularly our visa processing system, in our country's border security program. I have a much longer statement, Mr. Chairman, which I would like your permission to submit for the record.

Mr. Chairman, the resolve of the Department of State and the Bureau of Consular Affairs to be full partners in the war against terrorism is stronger than ever. In my testimony today, Mr. Chairman, I will describe what we have been doing to make our consular name check systems the best in the world and our plans to make them even better in the future. I will also address the procedures for visa issuance and the scope of the Department's data sharing with intelligence and law enforcement communities.

I can say with confidence that we are using today a state-of-the-art visa name check system, and we continue to seek and explore new technologies to expand our capabilities. If there is one thought that I can leave with the Subcommittee today, it is that any name check system is and will be only as good as the information we receive to put into it.

Let me begin by noting that all visa cases are processed using the automated name check system, which prompts the name check through the Department of State's centralized lookout system known as CLASS. A consular officer must review all hits before the case can be formally approved for printing. There is no override to this procedure. Simply stated, it is not possible to issue a visa unless the name check has been completed and reviewed by an officer.

The Department also has in place special headquarters clearance procedures for nationals of certain countries, including students, such as those on the State Sponsors of Terrorism list, as well as for those whose planned travel raises concerns about unauthorized access to sensitive technologies.

Once approved, a visa containing numerous safety features and a digitized photo is placed in the alien's passport. I should point out that the period of visa validity has nothing to do with the period for which the alien may remain in the United States. A visa permits the alien to apply for entry to the United States. Only INS may authorize such entry and determine the alien's length of stay.

Now, let me briefly describe our visa name check database. CLASS, which stands for Consular Lookout and Support System, contains about 5.7 million names concerning foreigners, most of which originate with visa applications at our consulates and embassies abroad. INS, DEA, the Department of Justice, and other Federal agencies also contribute to our system. We in turn have provided approximately 500,000 lookout records to other agencies through real-time electronic links to the Interagency Border Inspection System, known as IBIS.

In the aftermath of the World Trade Center bombing in 1993, the Bureau of Consular Affairs funded a counterterrorism tool known as TIPOFF. This utilizes sensitive intelligence and law enforcement information from the CIA, the NSA, FBI, and our overseas posts concerning known or suspected terrorists.

The TIPOFF staff screens all incoming intelligence reports and other sources of information for the names and biographic data of known and suspected terrorists. Permission is obtained from the relevant agencies to declassify identifying data of suspected terrorists, and then that data is entered into CLASS at IBIS.

The Visas Viper program is another integral part of TIPOFF. The Visas Viper staff, in close coordination with the Bureau of Consular Affairs, solicits information on suspected terrorists from overseas posts for inclusion into the database. Beginning in 1996, with the help of Congress through retained machine-readable visa fees, Consular Affairs undertook a major modernization of our systems. By 2001, all visa data collected abroad, including photographs of the applicants, is being replicated to the Consular Consolidated Database and is made available to posts abroad. This year we deployed a pilot program to share limited non-immigrant visa data with INS inspectors at the port of entry at Newark, and we are very pleased that INS will soon expand use of this replicated data to all ports of entry. This will provide each INS inspector with a photo to compare with the person in front of them, a system cheaper than fingerprints and just as effective.

The Consular Lookout and Support System is modern and extendable. Our name check system remains robust because we continue to upgrade it. Allow me to outline a few of the initiatives that we have underway right now.

For many years, we have sought access to FBI criminal data on aliens applying for non-immigrant visas. I am very grateful to Members of Congress that legislation has been introduced that would provide us this data. I particularly want to thank you, Mr. Chairman, Senator Brownback, and others on the Subcommittee for introducing S. 1452 on September 21st.

I realize that my time is almost out, and—

Chairman KENNEDY. This is very important.

Ms. RYAN. Should I just continue?

Chairman KENNEDY. Please.

Ms. RYAN. I don't want to take too long.

We will also soon introduce improved field backup name check systems for use when telecommunication links are interrupted, and by summer 2002, every visa-issuing post will have a local backup that closely approaches the abilities of the CLASS mainframe.

Photographs are key to our exploration of biometrics. Because every visa application already contains a photograph, we capture a biometric identifier on all applicants right now. For this reason, we have for some time been investigating the use of facial recognition technology for identification purposes.

Pilots at our posts in India and Nigeria have proved very promising, and in late August, we launched a pilot at the Kentucky Consular Center aimed at detecting invalid diversity visa applications. We will soon test the abilities of facial recognition software to compare visa applicants to a sample database of photographs of suspected terrorists. We seek to expand the pool of such photographs through liaison with other Government agencies. We are also consulting with private sector users of facial recognition technology.

We will also soon complete field-testing a new, more secure nonimmigrant visa and design a machine-readable, secure immigrant visa that will, in conjunction with the data-share program, virtually eliminate photo substitution. We are also planning to develop a forensic documents lab to give us an independent capability to detect and counter fraudulent or counterfeit U.S. and foreign visas and passports.

Mr. Chairman, all of these initiatives, past, present, and future, have been made possible because of a very wise decision by the Congress a few years ago to permit us to retain machine-readable visa fees. Since 1994, when we were given the authorization to charge and retain these fees, we have spent every penny sensibly and judiciously. We continue to rely on MRV fees, as we call the machine-readable visa fees, to finance the salary and basic benefits of virtually all American employees who provide consular services. Permanent and uncapped MRV fees are essential to continuing our efforts to enhance our border security program.

Mr. Chairman, in our free society, we must continue to improve the security of our borders while keeping our hearts, our minds, and our economy open to new ideas, new people, and new markets. CA has been and will continue to be a full partner in the battle against terrorism.

I close with the point that I made at the outset. We cannot be the effective outer ring of border security if we don't get information on people who seek to harm our country from intelligence and law enforcement agencies. Information sharing is key to the protection of our Nation.

Thank you, Mr. Chairman, and members of the Committee for allowing me to appear before you today. I will be pleased to try to answer any questions you may have.

[The prepared statement of Ms. Ryan follows:]

81-651 D-2

STATEMENT OF MARY A. RYAN, ASSISTANT SECRETARY FOR CONSULAR AFFAIRS, DEPARTMENT OF STATE

Mister Chairman and Members of the Committee:

Thank you for the opportunity to appear before you today to explain the role of the Bureau of Consular Affairs, and most particularly our visa processing system, in this country's border security program. I only wish, Mr. Chairman, that the context for this hearing could be different. In that case I could open these remarks by saying how happy I am to appear before you, because I am proud of the systems we have developed over the past several years and that we work very hard to improve each and every day. I would convey again my appreciation for the help that the Congress has given the Department to improve our consular systems by allowing us to retain machine-readable visa (MRV) fees. However, I appear before you today keenly aware of the terrible tragedy that befell our country and all civilized countries on September 11.

In my testimony, Mr. Chairman, I will outline for you what we have been doing to make our consular systems the best in the world and our plans to make those systems even better in the future. During my tenure as Assistant Secretary, the Bureau of Consular Affairs (CA) has been continually engaged in efforts to design, deploy, and improve the systems that help flag for our consular officers terrorists and criminals among visa applicants. I can say with confidence that ours is a state-of-the-art system that functions as it was designed. At the same time, we continue to seek and exploit new technologies to strengthen our capabilities. If there is any single point I can leave with the Committee, it is that that any namecheck system is and will be only as good as the information we receive to put in it.

VISA PROCESSING

I will first focus on non-immigrant visa processing and explain briefly how applicants are processed so that you will understand the environment in which out systems operate. Applicants for non-immigrant visas submit a written application, with a passport and photo, for adjudication by a commissioned consular officer or other designated U.S. citizen. Locally engaged staff assist in visa processing but are not authorized to approve and issue visas.

Visa applications are processed using sophisticated automated systems. Data entry automatically prompts a namecheck through the Department of State's centralized lookout system (CLASS, the details of which I will discuss later in my testimony). A consular officer must review all hits before the case can be formally approved for printing. There is no override for this feature; it is not possible to print a visa unless a namecheck has been completed and reviewed by an officer.

Consular officers evaluate applications by looking at the full range of criteria established by U.S. immigration law. They review the credibility of professed plans for travel to the U.S. For most visas, applicants must establish that they intend to visit the U.S. only temporarily, are qualified for the visa classification sought, and will undertake only activities consistent with the particular visa status. Applicants must also establish that they are not otherwise ineligible to receive a visa under one of the specific grounds of ineligibility in the Immigration and Nationality Act, including terrorism, drug trafficking and alien smuggling.

In addition to namecheck results, consular officers use a combination of experience, knowledge of local economic, political and cultural conditions, and common sense to evaluate applications. Supporting documentation may be solicited and reviewed as needed. When there are specific signs of fraud or deception, an investigation may be conducted using consular anti-fraud resources.

The ever-growing numbers of visa applications has meant that consular officers must reach decisions in individual cases rapidly. To assist them in doing so, our namecheck technology provides results in real-time. We have used outside linguistic experts to make our search criteria for "hits" as helpful as possible. We have instituted sophisticated Arabic and Russian/Slavic algorithms to identify names regardless of transliteration variations, and are presently developing a similar algorithm for Hispanic names.

Once approved, a visa containing numerous security features and a digitized photo is placed in the alien's passport. The maximum period of visa validity is ten years for multiple entries. The validities of different types of non-immigrant visas are determined on the basis of reciprocity with each foreign government. I should point out, Mr. Chairman, that the period of visa validity has nothing to do with the period for which an alien may remain in the United States. A visa permits an alien to apply for entry to the U.S., but only the INS may authorize such entry and determine the alien's length of stay.

Visa data, including photos and pertinent biographic data, is electronically forwarded to the Consolidated Consular Database maintained in Washington. This database also contains information on refused applications.

Immigrant visas are for persons intending to reside permanently in the United States. U.S. citizens and legal permanent resident aliens, as well as prospective employers, file with the INS petitions on behalf of certain relatives and employees. A special element of U.S. immigration law is the Diversity Visa (DV) for which "winners" are chosen by lottery. Like non-immigrant visa applicants, immigrant visa and DV applicants must undergo namechecks. In addition, an FBI employee at the National Visa Center does a National Criminal Information Center (NCIC) criminal history check of these applicants.

I should note that, while immigrants are covered by NCIC screening, non-immigrants are not. I'll return to the solution to this problem, which I hope is imminent, in the context of our namecheck system.

THE NAMECHECK SYSTEM

Integral to visa processing is the namecheck system. CA is well aware of the importance of sharing and receiving critical intelligence and criminal data from intelligence and law enforcement agencies. In addition to ensuring that no visa is issued without a namecheck, we have worked hard over the past decade to deliver more information from other agencies to our visa officers via the namecheck system.

Our lookout database, the Consular Lookout and Support System (CLASS), contains about 5.7 million records on foreigners, most of which originate with the visa application process at our consulates and embassies overseas. A variety of federal agencies contribute lookouts to our system. INS has provided over one million records, and DEA about 330,000. Customs is working with us to provide 20,000 or more lookouts from its serious drug violator records by the end of this year. We in turn provide Customs, INS and other agencies using the Interagency Border Inspection System (IBIS) with approximately 500,000 lookout records through a real-time electronic link.

We also provide our officers, and the INS, with data on lost and stolen foreign passports to prevent the use of such passports by impostors.

TIPOFF AND VISAS VIPER

In the aftermath of the 1993 World Trade Center bombing, the Bureau of Consular Affairs—as part of the Department of State's border security program—funded a border security and counterterrorism tool known as TIPOFF. It was developed, and is managed, by the Bureau of Intelligence and Research (INR), utilizing sensitive intelligence and law enforcement information from the CIA, NSA, FBI and our overseas posts concerning known or suspected terrorists. TIPOFF's objective is to detect these individuals either as they apply for visas overseas, or as they attempt to pass through U.S., Canadian, and Australian border entry posts. (Data-sharing programs were implemented with Canada in 1997, and with Australia in 2000.)

The TIPOFF staff in INR screens all incoming intelligence reports, embassy cables and other sources of information for those documents containing the names and biographic data of known or suspected terrorists. Following strict procedures approved by the respective intelligence and law enforcement agencies, permission is obtained to declassify names, nationalities, passport numbers and dates of birth of suspected terrorists. This data is then entered into CLASS and the INS and Custom Service's IBIS system. Consular officers overseas encounter "hits" based on TIPOFF data in the regular course of their work. The CLASS database contains over 48,000 such records. TIPOFF has passed approximately 23,000 records to INS and other inspection services at ports of entry via IBIS, which uses a higher standard of biographic data for its entries.

The Visas Viper program is an integral part of TIPOFF. The TIPOFF/Viper staff works in close coordination with CA to solicit information about suspected terrorists from overseas posts. This data is included in the TIPOFF database and watchlisted in CLASS and IBIS. A procedural adjunct to the Visas Viper program, called TIPPIX, incorporates terrorists' photographs into the TIPOFF and IBIS databases.

TIPOFF performs the following important functions:

- t helps preclude the inadvertent issuance of visas to terrorists whose names are known to intelligence and law enforcement agencies;
- It warns embassies and consulates that certain applicants may pose a security risk;
- It alerts intelligence and law enforcement agencies that a suspected terrorist is applying for a visa;

- It provides a means for informed decisions to be made on whether to issue a visa for operational or other policy considerations, or deny the application;
- It enables INS and Customs to detect suspected terrorists who may have obtained a visa prior to being watchlisted in CLASS, or who are attempting to enter the U.S. through the Visa Waiver Program (VWP);
- And it provides operational opportunities at border entry points through use of "silent hits" or other handling codes.

We are also comparing new TIPOFF hits in the Consular Lookout and Support System with visa issuance information in the Consolidated Consular Database, to determine if a subject of derogatory information was issued a visa before the hit was created.

SECURITY ADVISORY OPINIONS

We also address cases posing potential security threats using Security Advisory Opinion procedures. We have concluded a series of agreements with law enforcement and national security agencies concerning categories of individuals of concern. Such persons are the subjects of a cable prepared by a consular officer and disseminated electronically to all appropriate agencies for an in-depth clearance.

The Department of State has designated Cuba, Iran, Iraq, Libya, North Korea, Sudan, and Syria as state sponsors of terrorism. Visa applications by officials and diplomats of these countries for the most part must be submitted to the Visa Office for review and an advisory opinion as to ineligibility before a visa can be issued. (This requirement does not presently extend to diplomatic/official visa applicants from Syria.) Non-official visa applicants from these countries are also subject to a wide range of special clearance procedures based on their background, the nature of their proposed visit, and the type of visa they are seeking.

Based on agreements with the FBI, we also maintain a variety of special clearance procedures—beyond the regular CLASS namecheck—for numerous other nationalities, including Afghanistan. The reasons for these special clearance procedures vary, but include concerns related to espionage, technology transfer, economic sanctions, and human rights violations.

In addition to these nationality-specific clearance requirements, we universally require special clearance for applicants of any nationality who are the subject of the most serious CLASS lookouts. We similarly require special clearance for applicants whose planned travel to the United States raises concerns about unauthorized access to sensitive technologies, even if there is no lookout entry for the individual. Consular officers are also asked to submit for a security advisory opinion any other cases that they feel raise security concerns, regardless of namecheck results.

THE CONSULAR CONSOLIDATED DATABASE

Our data-sharing efforts are not, however, limited to the namecheck system. We are now delivering more information to our visa officers via a globalized database of visa records. Beginning in 1996, thanks to the help of Congress with retained MRV fees, Consular Affairs undertook major modernization of our systems. By March 2001, all visa data collected abroad was being replicated to the Consular Consolidated Database. In May 2001, we made the Consular Consolidated Database available to all our visa officers abroad. The photo and details of visa issuance, once only available locally to the post taking action, are now available in real-time to all visa offices worldwide. Visas can be checked at any point in the issuance process against all issued and refused visas worldwide, and consular management in Washington now has access to up-to-the-minute information about visa and passport issuance around the world.

DATA-SHARING WITH THE INS AND OTHER FEDERAL INSPECTION SERVICES

We are working to widen the flow of information to relevant Federal Inspection Services. We are mindful of the challenges that INS faces in inspecting millions of foreign visitors at ports of entry. We have a number of initiatives underway to share additional information with INS in order to improve border security. As I mentioned earlier, the Consolidated Consular Database allows us to make visa information, including digital non-immigrant visa photographs, immediately available both in Washington and at all consular sections worldwide. We want INS to be able to make good use of this data, in particular photos of each individual who has been issued a visa.

Since the mid-1990's, State and INS have had a cooperative program which has resulted in State forwarding to INS, for use at ports of entry, electronic data on 55%

of all immigrant visa recipients. The two agencies have cooperated in exchanging information at all stages of the immigrant visa process, from approving petitions to issuing legal permanent residence cards. We are about to make certain software changes that should allow complete sharing of immigrant visa information with INS within the next year.

The Department is prepared to share all of its replicated non-immigrant visa files with INS as soon as the Service is ready to receive it. Towards that end, in July 2001, we deployed a pilot program to share limited non-immigrant visa data with INS inspectors at Newark and with the INS forensic document lab. The program was expanded to Miami in September, and INS plans to make the data available to all ports of entry over the next several months. We look forward to the time when we can share all of our replicated files with all INS ports of entry, as they will give INS inspectors near real-time access to data that will allow them to better detect fraud and facilitate legitimate travelers. In the meantime, INS inspectors have access to our electronic visa data via telephone contact with the Visa Office.

LOOKING AHEAD: IMPROVING AND EXTENDING OUR SYSTEMS

The Bureau of Consular Affairs has staff specifically dedicated to technical development to ensure we maintain state-of-the-art tools for adjudicating visas. The Consular Lookout and Support System is modern and extendible. Our namecheck system remains robust because we continue to upgrade it. We are committed and are actively working to expand datasharing with INS, other federal inspection services and law enforcement agencies.

A. GAINING ACCESS TO FBI NCIC III DATA

We need access to FBI criminal record data (NCIC III) on aliens to assist consular officers in their adjudication of visa applications and have been seeking authority for such access for many years. We already screen our immigrant applicants using FBI information and want to do the same for non-immigrant applicants. We envision a system of index records on aliens (excluding all U.S. citizens and legal permanent residents) that is added directly to the CLASS lookout system and that will signal there may be derogatory FBI information on an applicant. I am grateful to Members of Congress that this legislation, which would also ensure INS access to such information, is included in the counter-terrorism measures now moving through Congress. Mr. Chairman, I also want to thank you, Senator Brownback, and others for introducing S. 1452, which would provide NCIC III access to us and INS.

B. SHORT-TERM IMPROVEMENTS TO VISA SYSTEMS

This winter we will introduce improved field backup namecheck systems. By summer 2002 we plan to deploy a "real time update" feature for these systems that will give every visa processing post a local back-up that closely approaches the abilities of the mainframe CLASS system.

Before the end of this year, we will modify our existing database of lost and stolen blank foreign passports to accommodate entries by Foreign Service posts of individual, foreign passports that are reported as lost or stolen. Lost and stolen passport data will continue to be shared with federal inspection agencies through IBIS.

Specific enhancements aimed at giving visa officers more detailed lookout information have been in the works over the past year. By spring 2002, we will deploy features in our nonimmigrant visa system that will increase the scope of data associated with our lookout entries. Using scanning, we will begin augmenting the lookouts with global, electronic access to refusal files (and photos) now kept at individual Foreign Service posts.

C. FACIAL RECOGNITION

As I have said, Mr. Chairman, every visa application contains a photograph, which means we already capture a biometric indicator for every applicant. Accordingly, we have been investigating the use of emerging facial recognition technology in the consular business process.

Evaluations comparing non-immigrant visa photos at posts in India and Nigeria proved promising in identifying impostors presenting fraudulent applications. In late August, we launched a pilot at the Kentucky Consular Center for Diversity Visas aimed at detecting invalid applications from persons working around our procedures. We will soon test the capability of facial recognition software to compare a sample database of photographs of suspected terrorists to those of visa applicants.

We seek to expand the pool of photographs available for this use through efforts with other USG agencies.

D. DOCUMENT SECURITY

We soon will complete field-testing a new, more secure non-immigrant visa. Laboratory tests have shown that it is much more tamper-resistant than the current version. We will also complete design of a machine-readable, secure immigrant visa that will, in conjunction with the data-share program, virtually eliminate photo-substitution. We will provide our consulates with special secure ink with which to cancel visas, so that efforts to "wash" or "recycle" genuine visas will be much more difficult.

We are planning to develop within the Bureau of Consular Affairs an independent capacity to detect and counter fraudulent or counterfeit U.S. and foreign visas and passports by creating a new office built around a forensic document laboratory. This office also would coordinate all Bureau efforts to assess biometrics technologies.

E. HUMAN RESOURCES

Using MRV fees, the Department currently funds the salaries and benefits of 2,130 full-time positions. MRV funds will also be required to increase consular staffing worldwide, to address growing demands in the visa adjudication process. We are committed to an effective training program for consular employees, including an intensive one-week training course for consular field officers on namecheck systems and linguistic concepts.

MACHINE-READABLE VISA FEES PROVIDE THE MEANS FOR IMPROVEMENTS

Mr. Chairman, all of these initiatives—past, present and future—have been made possible because of a very wise decision by Congress a few years ago to permit us to retain machine-readable visa (MRV) fees. Since 1994, we have spent every penny of these fees sensibly and judiciously. As I mentioned, the Bureau of Consular Affairs relies upon MRV fees to finance the salary and basic benefits of virtually all American employees who provide worldwide consular services as well as to make improvements to our systems. Permanent and uncapped MRV fees are essential to continuing our efforts to enhance the nation's Border Security Program. With this funding authority, we can ensure we have sufficient personnel to cover staffing and training gaps and to help meet peak season workloads. We can also adjust staffing to compensate for additional anticipated steps in the visa adjudication process and other changes to increase security.

This funding allowed us to modernize our consular systems, and some of our future proceeds will go into further system upgrades, such as the scanning of our refusal files to augment lookout information. Other major expenditures looming include establishing additional back-up capabilities for the sophisticated automated systems that support both CLASS and the Consolidated Consular Database.

The level of resources available to federal border agencies greatly affects our progress, particularly in interagency sharing of visa information. We must continue to work closely with other agencies on data-sharing to ensure full access to information for consular officers. We are anxious to provide visa data to federal inspection services and would like to see more rapid progress. Modernization of other agencies' systems—including more modern protocols in data exchange and more secure, flexible connectivity—is key to significant progress. We actively participate in the Border Agency Partnership (formerly IBIS), which aims to tackle these problems.

CLOSING

Mr. Chairman, we live in a free and open society. These characteristics, so precious to all Americans, make our country a magnet to those who seek greater political, economic and social opportunities, as well as a target for those who hate us and seek to do us harm. We must continue improving the security of our borders while keeping our hearts and our economy open to new people, ideas and markets. CA has been and will continue to be a full partner in the battle against terrorism. Although the freedom and openness we value so much make totally foolproof systems virtually impossible, I am confident that our current system is state-of-the-art and functions as it was designed. I am also confident that we are on the right track with our efforts to find new technologies and institute data-sharing arrangements with other agencies.

I close, Mr. Chairman, with the point I made at the outset of these remarks—the effectiveness and success of our systems rely not only on the quantity, but also on the quality and timeliness of the information that goes into it.

Thank you, Mr. Chairman, and members of the Committee, for permitting me to share my thoughts with you today. I would now be pleased to answer any questions you have for me.

Chairman KENNEDY. Very good, very helpful.

Ambassador?

STATEMENT OF LINO GUTIERREZ, ACTING ASSISTANT SECRETARY OF STATE FOR WESTERN HEMISPHERE AFFAIRS, DEPARTMENT OF STATE, WASHINGTON, D.C.

Mr. GUTIERREZ. Thank you, Mr. Chairman.

Mr. Chairman and members of the Committee, thank you for the opportunity to appear before you to discuss the areas of cooperation between the United States and the countries of the Western Hemisphere, in particular Canada and Mexico, in strengthening and securing our mutual borders.

The Western Hemisphere, perhaps more than any region in the world, has benefited from the free flow of trade, people, and ideas, and the U.S. has been a natural focus of that flow. What the U.S. Government has discovered in the past month, however, is that this flow, in addition to creating a natural commonality of interest, has also created a need to work closely together to better secure our mutual borders against terrorists and other criminals. We agree that strengthening the security of our borders has become an indispensable part of the Nation's efforts to prevent future terrorist attacks.

Most importantly, our shared border with Canada to the North and Mexico to the South represents our greatest challenge: how to effectively guard against terrorism. Both Mexico and Canada are working closely with the United States to address these challenges. Our cooperation with Mexico on border security has been a priority for many years. Even before the September 11th attacks, our efforts at working together on border security this year had intensified following the President's February trip to Mexico to meet with President Fox. Border security and safety are one of the pillars of the High Level Working Group on Migration, and both Secretary Powell and Attorney General Ashcroft have been closely engaged in the issue with their Mexican counterparts since April. Their efforts products renewed vigor in bilateral cooperation at identifying and dismantling alien smuggling rings in Mexico, increased intelligence sharing at the border between the U.S. and Mexican law enforcement agencies, and by means of the border liaison mechanism, resulted in improved cooperation through increased personal contact by officials on both sides of the border. The Fox administration has shown consistently a willingness to work with us in ways not imagined as possible just a couple of years ago. The Government of Mexico responded immediately to the September 11th terrorist attacks with concrete actions to tighten border security and to cooperate with U.S. law enforcement officials.

I have submitted a written statement to the Committee for the record which includes examples of Mexican cooperation. Right now I'll mention a couple of examples.

The Government of Mexico offered full cooperation with FAA authorities to survey all international airports in Mexico. The Mexican Government instituted special visa screening procedures for nationals of over 50 countries. No visa can be issued without advance approval from officials in Mexico City.

The cooperation from Mexican agencies has been active and outstanding. Every law enforcement, military, and intelligence entity has worked tirelessly with us. There have been dozens of leads initiated by Mexican authorities. An embassy agency head described the level of cooperation as "extraordinary."

We had been working with Mexican authorities prior to September 11th to encourage them to review and tighten their policies in the transit of third-country nationals through Mexico. The Mexicans have made progress in certain areas, particularly on their southern border, with stemming the flow of immigrants transiting Mexico to the U.S. While the overwhelming majority of those who attempt to enter the U.S. do so for economic reasons, we have insisted that Mexico do more in this area to ensure that potential malafide migrants do not take advantage of alien smuggling networks to the U.S.

Since September 11th, Canada has become a key partner in the war on terrorism. On the day of the attacks, Canada allowed some 245 international flights headed for the United States to land at its airports. The upwards of 27,000 passengers, including many American citizens, were cared for by the Canadian officials and the Canadian people for several days. Currently, significant Canadian military assets, including a four-ship task force, are being folded into our military response. Canada has been a staunch and forthcoming ally.

Again, my written statement lists a number of examples of Canadian cooperation. I will mention a few.

On October 15th, the Canadian Government introduced in parliament sweeping anti-terrorism legislation which gives police more authority to crack down on terrorists and cut off fundraising for suspected terrorist groups.

On October 12th, the Canadian Government announced a $55 million (Canadian dollars) boos in the budget of the Royal Canadian Mounted Police to create new border and national security teams, update forensic technology and databases, and increase protection of key sites.

Another $49 million package was announced in Ottawa last week that will provide for 100 additional immigration officers at border points, increased efforts to deport illegal entrants, and new fraud-resistant identity cards for legal immigrants.

Our cooperation with Canada on shared border security is extensive and in-depth. There are six bilateral fora currently, including Border Vision, the Shared Border Accord, the Canada–U.S. Partnership, the Cross–Border Crime Forum, the Bilateral Consultative Group on Counter–Terrorism. All these will be meeting in the near future to discuss additional steps.

We interact daily with Canadian ministries, parliament, the media, and the Canadian people. We have redoubled our efforts since September 11th, and those efforts are paying dividends.

The countries of the Western Hemisphere have demonstrated that they are important allies in the effort to condemn and combat terrorism. Many countries of the hemisphere—most importantly Canada and Mexico, who share our physical borders—are working cooperatively with the U.S. to examine policies and develop efforts to strengthen border security. More needs to be done throughout the hemisphere to adopt modern investigative techniques, improve airport security, encourage a sharing of information, cooperate in law enforcement and financial investigation efforts, and monitor and suppress money laundering and alien smuggling, which are criminal activities that also provide resources for the terrorists. We are urging all countries of the hemisphere to sign and ratify the 12 international conventions that address terrorist threats and to implement fully the terms of the UN Security Council Resolution 1373 with respect to blocking terrorists' access to fund. We are a party to ten of these conventions and have signed two: the 1998 Convention for the Suppression of Terrorist Bombings, and the 1999 Convention on the Suppression of Financing of Terrorism Crimes. We are pleased that the Senate Foreign Relations Committee is receiving testimony on these two remaining convention on Thursday, and we urge the Senate to review and ratify them expeditiously.

Our hemispheric commitment to confront terrorism will be demonstrated by the concrete measures we take as sovereign governments and as a community of governments to arm ourselves against this worldwide threat. We will continue to call on our hemispheric neighbors to join us in our counterterrorism efforts and in sending a unified message that these criminal activities are not welcome in our neighborhood.

Thank you.

[The prepared statement of Mr. Gutierrez follows:]

STATEMENT OF LINO GUTIERREZ, ACTING ASSISTANT SECRETARY, BUREAU OF WESTERN HEMISPHERE AFFAIRS

Mr. Chairman and Members of the Committee:

Thank you for the opportunity to appear before you today to discuss the areas of cooperation between the United States and the countries of the Western Hemisphere—in particular Canada and Mexico—in strengthening and securing mutual borders.

In the aftermath of the September 11 terrorist attacks, the countries of the Americas have responded strongly and positively against international terrorism and in solidarity with the United States, and have supported our efforts to construct an international counterterrorism coalition. A tragic testimony of the degree to which our fates are linked is the list of thirty of the Hemisphere's thirty-four nations which lost citizens in the September 11 events—among those nations directly affected, El Salvador counts 121 dead and missing, the Dominican Republic 42, Canada 24, and Mexico 18.

The Western Hemisphere, perhaps more than any region in the world, has benefited from the free flow of trade, people and ideas, and the U.S. has been a natural focus of that flow. What the USG has discovered in the past month however, is that this flow—in addition to creating a natural commonality of interest—has also created a need to work closely together to better secure our mutual borders against terrorists and other criminals. We agree that strengthening the security of our borders has become an indispensable part of the nation's efforts to prevent future terrorist attacks.

Expressions of solidarity and sympathy are being matched by concrete actions by the nations of the hemisphere. Hemispheric governments are beefing up security measures, sharing intelligence, and looking at ways to improve border security. For example, on October 12, the Caribbean (CARICOM) heads of state issued an anti-terrorism declaration pledging to put in place the "necessary measures to comply with new international safety regulations on planes, at airports arid sea ports." Additionally, the OAS Inter-American Committee Against Terrorism (CICTE), which met in a special session on Monday, October 15, is coordinating OAS member states' efforts to reduce the ability of terrorist groups to operate in the hemisphere, including enhancing border cooperation and travel document security measures. As part of this cooperation, CICTE member states have been briefed by top U.S. and Canadian government experts in the areas of counterterrorism, terrorist financing, and border controls.

Most importantly, our shared border with Canada to the north and Mexico to the south, which covers a distance of over 6,000 miles, facilitates—under normal conditions—the legal crossing of approximately 1.6 million people and almost 2 billion U.S. dollars per day in trade with Canada and Mexico. Although this impressive level of activity demonstrates the positive effects of trade and globalization, it also represents our greatest challenge: how to effectively guard against terrorism. Both Mexico and Canada are working closely with the U.S. to address these challenges.

MEXICO

Our cooperation with Mexico on border security has been a priority issue for many years. Even before the September 11 attacks, our efforts at working together on border security this year had intensified following the President's February trip to Mexico to meet with President Fox. Border security and safety are one of the pillars of the High Level Working Group on Migration, and both Secretary Powell and Attorney General Ashcroft have been closely engaged in the issue with their Mexican counterparts since April. Their efforts produced renewed vigor in bilateral cooperation at identifying and dismantling alien smuggling rings in Mexico, increased intelligence sharing at the border between U.S. and Mexican law enforcement agencies, and, by means of the Border Liaison Mechanisms, resulted in improved cooperation through increased personal contact by officials on both sides of the border. The Fox administration has shown consistently a willingness to work with us in ways not imagined as possible just a couple of years ago. The government of Mexico responded immediately to the September 11 terrorist attacks with concrete actions to tighten border security and to cooperate with U.S. law enforcement officials.

Some examples:

- Mexican authorities stopped two U.S. residents on September 12 entering at Mexicali with suspicious documents.
- Mexican immigration picked up 30 individuals in Tijuana and sent them to Mexico City for questioning.
- An additional four people were picked up September 17 in Durango for questioning.
- Mexican authorities worked closely with their U.S. government counterparts inside Mexico to investigate evidentiary leads such as an ice pick on a plane from the U.S., a suspicious piece of luggage with Arabic tapes and documents, and reports of suspicious crop dusters near the U.S. border.
- The government of Mexico offered full cooperation with FAA authorities to survey all international airports in Mexico.
- The Mexican government instituted special visa issuance screening procedures for nationals of over 50 countries. No visas can be issued without advance approval from officials in Mexico City.

The cooperation from Mexican agencies has been active and outstanding. Every law enforcement, military and intelligence entity has worked tirelessly with us. There have been dozens of leads initiated by Mexican authorities. An Embassy agency head described the level of cooperation as "extraordinary."

We had been working with Mexican authorities prior to September 11 to encourage them to review and tighten their policies on the transit of "third country" nationals through Mexico. The Mexicans have made progress in certain areas, particularly on their southern border, with stemming the flow of immigrants transiting Mexico to the U.S. While the overwhelming majority of those who attempt to enter the U.S. do so for economic reasons, we have insisted that Mexico do more in this area to ensure that potential malafide migrants do not take advantage of alien smuggling networks to enter the U.S.

As part of this effort, the Government of Mexico has been proactive in identifying and disrupting rings of alien smugglers on the U.S. border and throughout Mexico.

CANADA

Since September 11, Canada has become a key partner in the war on terrorism. On the day of the attacks, Canada allowed some 245 international flights, headed for the United States, to land at its airports. The upwards of 27,000 thousand passengers, including many American citizens, were cared for by the Canadian government and the Canadian people for several days. On the Friday following the attack, some 100,000 Canadians attended an official memorial ceremony on Ottawa's Parliament Hill to pay tribute to the victims. Currently, significant Canadian military assets, including a four-ship task force, are being folded into our military response. Canada has been a staunch and forthcoming ally.

Other examples of Canadian cooperation include:

- Working hand in hand with us on investigating literally thousands of leads in the wake of the September 11 terrorism attacks.
- On September 12, Canadian border guards arrested a man carrying several bogus pilot licenses as he tried to enter Canada from the U.S. Canadian officials immediately handed him over to U.S. authorities.
- Canadian authorities detained and turned over to us a passenger on a flight diverted from the U.S. to Canada on September 11 after he was found to be in the possession of several airline uniforms.
- Canadian officials are also working closely with their U.S. counterparts to investigate the discovery of box-cutter knives found aboard an Air Canada flight scheduled to fly from Toronto to New York, but grounded at the last minute on September 11.
- In-depth security interviews were imposed for refugee claimants in the weeks after September 11.
- On October 12, the Canadian Government announced a S55 million (Canadian dollars) boost in the budget of the Royal Canadian :Mounted Police to create new border and national security teams, update forensic technology and databases, and increase protection of key sites.
- Another $49 million package announced in Ottawa last week will provide for 100 additional immigration officers at border points, increased efforts to deport illegal entrants, and new fraud-resistant identity cards for legal immigrants.
- Canada has announced airport improvements worth USDS60 million for more bomb detectors, staff, and modernized computer systems.
- The Canadian Government has also introduced in Parliament new anti-terrorism legislation giving police more authority to crack down on terrorists and cut off fundraising for suspected terrorist groups.

Our cooperation with Canada on shared border security is extensive and in-depth. Coordination is based in six bilateral fora—Border Vision. whose overall goal is a bilateral, strategic approach to migration which will strengthen the integrity of the border through information and intelligence sharing, policy coordination, joint overseas operations and border cooperation; the Shared Border Accord, whose goal is to develop new and innovative programs that will facilitate bilateral trade and the movement of people; the Canada-U.S. Partnership, announced by the two countries' heads of government in 1999 to look at cross-border issues and provide a framework for non-federal stakeholders to air their views; the Cross-Border Crime Forum to address crime issues; the Bilateral Consultative Group on Counter-Terrorism to bring both countries' top counter-terrorism experts together annually; and the Integrated Border Enforcement Team, a bilateral, multi-agency law enforcement group of police, customs and immigration officials.

In all of these areas, the Bureau of Western Hemisphere Affairs' most appropriate role is advocating and coordinating policy with the highest levels of Canadian political and policy decision-making. We advocate forcefully for U.S. government policies through our Embassy in Ottawa and our seven consulates across Canada. We interact daily with Canadian ministries, Parliament, the media, and the Canadian people. We have redoubled our efforts since September 11. And those efforts are paying dividends. Our Canadian friends have recognized that there are some weaknesses in their immigration law and have introduced legislation to, among other provisions, make refugee/asylum claimants excludable even if they are merely suspected of terrorist ties, and given Canadian law enforcement increased access to advance passenger information on incoming flights. And, on October 15, the Canadian government introduced in Parliament sweeping anti-terrorist legislation, which includes giving police authority to tap phones and electronic mail, and makes it a crime to harbor a terrorist. It also takes the step of making it a crime to raise funds or participate in activities of terrorist groups.

The ability of the Canadian government to secure its homeland will only help us in securing our homeland. A higher level of confidence about who Canada is admitting at its ports of entry would assist us greatly in allowing us to focus our northern border resources where and how they will do the most good. Canada feels the same way about us. Even greater information and intelligence sharing, and the development and sharing of new technologies, will allow both countries to focus more on the commonality of our immigration efforts. With 1.2 billion dollars in trade crossing our mutual border daily and 200 million people annually, the goal should be to foster this invaluable flow of people and goods while also increasing safeguards against threats. We are confident that our Canadian partners share this goal, and stand ready to work with us to make it happen.

CONCLUSION

The countries of the Western Hemisphere have demonstrated that they are important allies in the effort to condemn and combat terrorism. In addition to the numerous expressions of condolence and solidarity, events in Washington (including the invocation of the Rio Treaty by States Parties at the OAS on September 19 and the extraordinary convocation of OAS foreign ministers on September 21) were important measures of our support within the hemisphere.

In addition. many countries in the hemisphere—most importantly Canada and Mexico who share our physical borders—are working cooperatively with the U.S. to examine policies and develop efforts to strengthen border security. More needs to be done throughout the hemisphere to adopt modern investigative techniques, improve airport security, encourage countries of the region to work among themselves to share information, cooperate in law enforcement and financial investigation efforts, and monitor and suppress money laundering and alien smuggling, which are criminal activities that also provide resources and logistic support for terrorists and other malefactors. We are urging all the countries of the hemisphere to sign and ratify the 12 international conventions that address terrorist threats and to implement fully the terms of UNSC Resolution 1373 with respect to blocking terrorists' access to funds. We are a party to ten of these conventions and have signed two: the 1998 Convention for the Suppression of Terrorist Bombings and the 1999 Convention on the Suppression of Financing of Terrorism Crimes. We are pleased that the Senate Foreign Relations Committee is receiving testimony on these two remaining Conventions on Thursday and we urge the Senate to review and ratify them expeditiously.

Our hemispheric commitment to confront terrorism will be demonstrated by the concrete measures we take as sovereign governments and as a community of governments to arm ourselves against this worldwide threat. We will continue to call on our hemispheric neighbors to join us in our counterterrorism efforts and in sending a unified message that these criminal activities are not welcome in our neighborhood.

Chairman KENNEDY. Thank you.

Mr. Ziglar?

STATEMENT OF JAMES W. ZIGLAR, COMMISSIONER, IMMIGRATION AND NATURALIZATION SERVICE, DEPARTMENT OF JUSTICE, WASHINGTON, D.C.

Mr. ZIGLAR. Mr. Chairman and members of the Committee, I appreciate the opportunity to appear today to talk about border control issues in the context of the anti-terrorist effort. Needless to say, Mr. Chairman, I am very pleased to be before this Committee. As you know, historically I have a great affection for this Committee, as you well know, going back to the 1960s when I worked up here in this Committee, and I am obviously, for other reasons, very interested in your work in my new role.

Chairman KENNEDY. It goes back to the 1965 Act of the elimination of the national origin quota system, the Asian Pacific triangle.

Mr. ZIGLAR. That is right.

Chairman KENNEDY. I remember. A very important piece of immigration legislation eliminating discrimination.

Mr. ZIGLAR. Exactly.

Chairman KENNEDY. We know that you have been interested in these issues for a long time.

Mr. ZIGLAR. Obviously, Mr. Chairman, I also was very pleased to be the Sergeant at Arms and am forever grateful for that opportunity.

I had a couple of questions this morning from the press that prompt me to say something that is not in my notes, but I think it is important to remember, particularly in the context of this Committee, this Subcommittee, and that is that the issue that we are facing in the country here is not an issue about immigration. It is an issue about evil. Immigrants are not terrorists. Immigrants are people who want to come to this country to share in this country and to contribute.

The people that we are talking about, the hijackers, they weren't immigrants. They were non-immigrants. They were people who were coming trying to visit our country to do damage. There are millions and millions and millions of people who want to come to this country not as immigrants but as visitors. And we have to control our borders to make sure that those kinds of people, obviously an immigrant, somebody who wants to emigrate to do harm, we obviously need to know who they are, too. But we need to keep this in the context that immigration is not a bad thing, that immigrants are not terrorists. There may be some among their groups, but we don't need to lump all immigrants into this, and I think that is an attitude that I see developing, at least among the press, based on the questions I am hearing. And I just think we need to keep that in context.

When I started this job 2 months ago, I was looking for a big challenge, but I had no idea that I was going to get the challenge that I face, the turn that has come. When the President gave me a goal or gave me some goals for this agency—and I think I talked to each one of you about taking this job—there were three things that really needed to be done: one was to restructure the organization in a way that it could fulfill its enforcement and service missions more appropriately and more efficiently; secondly was to modernize the management processes and structures so that it could carry out those missions; and thirdly was to modernize and synchronize the technology infrastructure of the INS so that it also could do a better job at carrying out its missions.

Well, I have to tell you, from my point of view the mission that was set before me before September 11th is exactly the same mission today, and that is, the only way we are going to help protect the American people from the kind of evil that we saw on September the 11th is to have a more efficient and effective government and to have a more efficient and efficiency Immigration and Naturalization Service.

I think it is worth noting that the INS bears a very heavy burden that most Americans don't realize. We share a responsibility at the ports of entry with the Custom Service and vetting people and things that come across those borders. But between those ports of entry, the 6,000 miles of border that we have, land border that we have in this country, the INS has sole responsibility for patrolling that.

People don't realize that we have more than 500 million—I think it was 530 million people cross our borders every year. That is a staggering number. And, frankly, about 350 million of them are non–U.S. citizens, so there are another 175 million U.S. citizens that cross. But 350 million non–U.S. citizens cross our borders every year. And most of the people come over here through visa waiver programs or other exemptions. So they never have shown up at one of Mary Ryan's places to get a visa. They come under other programs.

Most Americans don't realize that we have got less than 5,000 inspectors throughout the entire world in the INS to process these hundreds of millions of people who want to come to this country. Most people don't realize that we have about 2,000 intelligence officers and investigators who are charged with the responsibility around the world of dealing with undocumented aliens, overstays, smuggling, human smuggling rings, and criminal aliens that are among us. That is 2,000 for a huge number of people.

As I noted, this is a very heavy burden to bear.

Without a doubt, the tragic events of September 11th have focused the Nation and the Congress on the management of our borders. I have got to tell you, Mr. Chairman, that the INS is a willing, enthusiastic, and cooperative partner in this fight against terrorism. I believe that we have the will, we have got the determination, and with your help we will have the human and other resources necessary to meet that challenge. But we are moving ahead. We are not waiting for people to tell us what to do.

For one thing, let me tell you that, first, we are going to present to you probably next week a reorganization plan at the INS. I am moving forward with those goals, notwithstanding what occurred on September 11th, and we are going to present to you a reorganization plan that has now been approved by the Attorney General personally. It is in the process of being approved at OMB, and it is substantial and it is significant in terms of the way we will do our business at the INS.

In the technology area, we are moving very rapidly to engage force multipliers so that we can do our job better. We are developing an enterprise architecture plan that is based upon a study and a design that we worked out with GAO. I might add that the GAO used us as a guinea pig to design and approach the enterprise architecture throughout the Government. We are the original organization that will be using this structure to design the enterprise architecture.

But we are not waiting for that plan to be in place in terms of developing our technology. We are presently going forward using an investment review board process, an interim technology enterprise architecture structure to start building our technology that will fit on this platform, that will be hopefully interrelated with all the other Government agencies.

Mr. Chairman, with your support—and you talked about the SEVIS system, and I know that is important to everyone on this panel. The SEVIS system is the student tracking system which I think was also known as CIPRIS at one point. It has been the product of a lot of controversy up until recently. There was a lot of opposition to it from the academic establishment. There was opposition in Congress because of the fees and that sort of thing. That is a system that, with your help, with some appropriations, we can get started moving that system forward, and we can beat the deadline or meet the deadline, certainly, that the Congress set originally of 2003.

Mr. Chairman, you mentioned in your opening remarks the number of institutions that are involved in that system or that can issue I–20s for students. That is a huge issue. There are almost 74,000 institutions in this country that can issue I–20s, and we have never really screened them out or done anything like to see who is it that is actually issuing I–20s and bringing students in.

I can tell you, last week I started the information-gathering process that we can start screening and qualifying these people. I think that is a huge issue, and it is something that we are very focused on.

Mr. Chairman, we are integrating our various enforcement databases into something called the ENFORCE system. One of the criticisms, and a legitimate criticism, of the INS and other institutions in our Government is that we have databases all over the place, but nobody knows what data the other people have, a bunch of stovepipes. That is true in the INS. There is no question about it.

We are in the process of developing an overall database, if you will, called ENFORCE where all of this information we have lodged in all these different places will go into that ENFORCE system.

We already have integrated that with our IDENT system, which is a biometric identification system. People get IDENT and other things confused. They think IDENT is a database. It is not. It is an identification system that tells us who this person is that we have in front of us; then what you need to know once you figure out who the person is, what do you know about that person. And that is what we have done. We have integrated those, and we are trying to integrate all of our database systems, and we are making a lot of progress at doing that.

The so-called IAFIS system, which is the FBI system, which is a ten-print I.D. system, is also being integrated with the IDENT system pursuant to the instructions of the Congress. We are making some pretty good progress on that. We are going to be rolling out our first transitional work station on the IDENT/IAFIS system. We will be doing that very shortly, and that will take us ultimately to an integration of those two systems.

The entry/exit system that you mentioned that I have been very interested in, again, we are on track to have that system up and running by the congressionally mandated 2003, and we are going to use the IBIS system, which Mary Ryan referred to, as our platform for the entry/exit system. That will be a very good tool for us in terms of tracking people who are in overstay status.

As I have mentioned a number of times, the idea that people that overstay, that we can somehow track them, given the number of people that come into this country, is pretty hard to do unless we want to put somebody on everybody who is in the country or if we want to plant a chip in their or something like that. That is not possible. But we do need better information about who these people are and the fact that they have overstayed, and that is what the entry/exit system will do.

With your help, we can complete the border crossing card system, and with your help, we can expand the IDENT system which has been stalled since the year 2000 because of some moratorium and some other things that have been imposed upon us.

Mary Ryan mentioned, Mr. Chairman, that we came to an agreement last week to deploy the Consolidated Consular Database to all of our ports of entry out of the State Department system. This is a good example of working together. That system, which is a facial recognition system or a digital photographic system, is going to be deployed, and it is going to be deployed within the next 3 months to all of our ports of entry. It will substantially enhance our ability to detect fraud and to figure out if the people we have in front of us are really the people who they say they are.

Mr. Chairman, just a couple of other things. I know my time has long since run out. We need to do some other things, and I have included a bunch of them in my testimony. But some of them are to substantially increase the number of our Border Patrol agents, our intelligence officers, and our investigators and our inspectors. We have got to have more of those people if we are going to do our job.

We need to require air carriers—and you mentioned this—to provide us with advance passenger information so that even before somebody boards, we know who is getting on that plane, or at least from the name point of view we know who is getting on that plane; and then after the plane takes off, to confirm who is on that plane so that by the time they get to a port of entry, we have some information that we can gather on those folks.

Finally—and this is extremely important, and Senator Cantwell mentioned this, and I can't emphasize it enough because I know Mary Ryan and I feel very strongly about this, and that is, cooperation among Government agencies, intelligence agencies, information-gathering agencies, and those kinds of agencies. The sharing of data and making that data available to all people interested in this process is absolutely critical for us to have a good line of defense against people who are coming into this country who want to do harm to our country.

Mr. Chairman, we have got to increase security. There is no question about that. But in doing that, we must not forget those things that made our country truly great. It is our openness to new ideas and to new people, a commitment to individual civil liberties, shared values, innovation, and the free market. If in response to the events of September 11th we sacrifice those things in search of security, the terrorists will have won. And in the end, we will be left with neither security nor freedom.

Thank you, Mr. Chairman. I appreciate it.

[The prepared statement of Mr. Ziglar follows:]

STATEMENT OF JAMES W. ZIGLAR, COMMISSIONER, IMMIGRATION AND NATURALIZATION SERVICE

Chairman and Members of the Committee, I want to thank you for the opportunity to testify on the topic of "Effective Immigration Controls to Deter Terrorism." I am always pleased to return to the Senate. I shall always be grateful for the opportunity I had to serve as the Senate Sergeant at Arms from November 1998 to August 2001.

Although I have served as Commissioner for only two months, I have not viewed that as a liability in responding to the tragic events of September 11, primarily because of the highly professional career public servants who have provided me with mature advice and assistance. These tragic events, however, have provided an opportunity for me to examine, with a fresh eye, the management, personnel, technology, and policy capabilities of the INS.

Steps to Improve Security

Even before September 11, we were examining how we can improve the INS, at all levels, and especially in the area of technology. We recognize that technology is a huge "force multiplier" that we must employ effectively at the INS if we are to accomplish our mission.

Pursuant to the mandates of the Clinger-Cohen legislation, in response to the recommendations of the General Accounting Office (GAO), and because it makes good business sense, the INS is currently in the process of developing its Enterprise Architecture. This project represents our long-term, strategically-oriented approach to accomplishing the information driven aspects of the INS mission. We began the planning for this project in October 2000 and I expect the final delivery of this project, the transition plan to our target architecture, to be ready at the beginning of the 3rd quarter of FY 2002. In addition, as part of our overall restructuring initiative, I encouraged our employees at all levels to think "outside the box" as to how we can better accomplish our mission. They responded with a number of creative ideas, some of which we are still evaluating. However, within the context of what is already known to be "doable" and effective, we are considering a series of measures that would strengthen our enforcement capabilities. We are working within the Administration to determine how to implement these measures. Some of our ideas are as follows:

Border Patrol

- As requested in the President's budget, increase the number of Border Patrol agents and support staff along the northern border, while not neglecting the continuing needs along the southwest border. Such increases should also include necessary facilities, infrastructure and vehicles.
- Provide additional agent support equipment and technology enhancements. Unfortunately, neither the Senate nor the House currently is funding the President's request at $20 million for "force multiplying technology."
- Expand access to biometric identification systems, such as IDENT.

Inspections

- In the Inspections area, as we proposed in our FY 2002 budget, we believe we should increase the number of Inspectors at our Ports of Entry.
- Require inspection of all International-to-International Transit Passengers (ITI) so that all travelers who arrive in the United States are inspected.

Informatton and Technology Initiatives

Require carriers to submit Advance Passenger Information before boarding passengers (whether the passenger is heading to the United States or attempting to depart the United States) to assist in preventing known or suspected terrorists, criminals, and inadmissible passengers from boarding.

Make Advance Passenger Information data widely available to law enforcement agencies, enhancing the ability to identify potential threats prior to departure from or arrival in the United States, as well as to prevent the departure of individuals who may have committed crimes while in the United States.

Implement the National Crime Information Center Interstate Identification Index (NCIC III) at all ports of entry so that aliens with criminal histories can be identified prior to or upon arrival in the United States. NCIC III should also be available at all consular posts, INS service centers and adjudication offices to help identify aliens who pose a potential threat.

Improve lookout system checks for the adjudications of applications at INS service centers.

Improve INS infrastructure and integration of all data systems so that data from all sources on aliens is accessible to inspectors, special agents, adjudicators, and other appropriate law enforcement agencies. This initiative is ongoing.

Personnel Issues

Waive the calendar-year overtime cap for INS employees to increase the number of staff-hours available by increasing the overtime hours people can work. This proposal is included in the Administration's Anti-Terrorism Bill.

81-651 D-3

OTHER INITIATIVES

Re-examine and potentially eliminate the Transit Without Visa Program (TWOV) and Progressive Clearance to prevent inadmissible international passengers from entering the United States.

Reassess the designation of specific countries in the Visa Waiver Program to ensure that proper passport policies are in place. This initiative will require the concurrence of and joint participation by the Department of State.

Explore alternative inspection systems that allow for facilitation of low risk travelers while focusing on high-risk travelers.

And review the present listing of designated ports of entry, in concert with the U.S. Customs Service, to eliminate unnecessary ports. This will allow the INS to deploy more inspectors to fewer locations making for a more efficient use of resources.

DATABASE IMPROVEMENTS

In addition to the measures cited above, I have instructed my staff to move forward expeditiously on two database improvement projects mandated by Congress. While neither is a panacea, both would be an improvement over the status quo. First, there has been much attention paid to student visas in recent weeks. Today, the INS maintains limited records on foreign students and is able to access that information on demand. However, the information is on old technology platforms that are insufficient for today's need for rapid access. That is why we are moving forward with the Student Exchange Visitor Information System (SEVIS), formerly known as CIPRIS. Objections, primarily by the academic establishment, have delayed its development and deployment. However, with the events of September 11, that objection has virtually disappeared. INS, with your help, will meet the Congress' date of January 2003 to start implementation of SEVIS with respect to all foreign nationals holding student visas. I hasten to add that there is a critical need to concurrently review and revise the process by which foreign students gain admission to the United States through the I-20 certification process as we build the system.

Second, substantial attention also has been paid to entry and exit data. Currently, the INS collects data on the entry and exit of certain visitors. The data, most of which is provided to the INS in paper form to meet our manifest requirements, first must be transferred by hand from paper to an electronic database. This is an extremely inefficient way of processing data which delays access to the data by weeks and months. Knowing who has entered and who has departed our country in real time is an important element in enforcing our laws. The Data Management Improvement Act, passed in 2000, requires the INS to develop a fully-automated integrated entry-exit data collection system and deploy this system at airports and seaports by the end of 2003, the 50 largest land ports of entry by the end of 2004, and completing the deployment to all other ports of entry by the end of 2005. The legislation also requires a private sector role to ensure that any systems developed to collect data do not harm tourism or trade.

The INS already uses limited airline and cruise line data that is now provided voluntarily as an integral part of the inspection process at airports and seaports. We will work closely with Congress, other agencies, and the travel industry in the coming months to expand our access to needed data and to enhance our use of that data to ensure border security and more complete tracking of arrivals and departures.

There has also been a great deal of focus on the databases used to identify persons who are inadmissible to the United States or who pose a threat to our country. The INS, the Customs Service, and the Department of State's Bureau of Consular Affairs have worked diligently over the past decade to provide our ports of entry and consular posts with access to data needed by our officers. The data contained in the National Automated Immigration Lookout System (NAILS), the Treasury Enforcement Communications System (TECS II), and the Consular Lookout and Support System (CLASS) are uniformly available to our ports of entry through a shared database called the Interagency Border Inspection System (IBIS) that is maintained on the U.S. Customs Service mainframe computer. Last week, I announced that INS and the Department of State have agreed to aggressively deploy the Consolidated Consular Database to INS ports-of-entry within the next three months. This will provide inspectors with the capability to verify rapidly and definitively the identity of visa-holders seeking admission to the United States. This new functionality will be provided to inspectors at ports-of-entry through the IBIS system.

Through IBIS, the officers at our ports of entry can also access limited data from the National Crime Information Center (NCIC). Immigration and Customs officers have long had the capability to check NCIC wanted persons data on a limited basis.

Only recently have immigration inspectors been authorized to routinely use NCIC criminal history data (NCIC III) to identify criminal aliens in advance of their arrival. This capacity now exists at two ports of entry. Before September 11, the INS was working to expand the availability of this valuable data source to additional locations. Legislation is being considered to ensure this expansion is successful. I strongly support this legislation.

Many people who cross our land borders do so with a Border Crossing Card (BCC). The INS and State Department have been working aggressively over the past several years to replace the old Border Crossing Cards with the new biometric "laser visa." Based on the statutory deadline, holders of the old BCC can no longer enter the country. The new BCC has many security features that make it a much more secure entry document.

Both at and between our ports of entry, the INS has used a fingerprint identification system known as IDENT to track immigration violators. This system has provided the INS with a significant capacity to identify recidivists and impostors. Congress has directed the Department of Justice to integrate IDENT with access to the FBI's automated fingerprint system, IAFIS, and we have been proceeding toward that objective with the FBI and under the Department's direction.

The Limits of Technology

There is no quick fix, technological or otherwise, to the problems we face. We must work with advanced technology and do all we can to improve our systems. But we should not mislead ourselves into thinking that technology alone can solve our problems. Technology must be coupled with a strong intelligence and information-gathering and distribution system if we are to leverage our resources and maximize our capabilities. That will require the seamless cooperation among the many government agencies involved.

It should be noted that more than five hundred million inspections are conducted at our ports of entry every year, and hundreds of millions of people enter the United States without visas, either because they are U.S. citizens, through visa waiver programs, or other exemptions from the normal visa process; the INS has only 4,775 Inspectors to process these hundreds of millions of visitors and approximately 2,000 investigators and intelligence agents throughout the country who are available to deal with persons who have entered illegally, are criminal aliens, or have overstayed their visas or otherwise have violated the terms of their status as visitors in the United States.

If we are to meet the challenges of the future, we need to make changes at the INS and we are in the process of making those changes. The structure of the organization and the management systems that we have in place are outdated and, in many respects, inadequate for the challenges we face. Our information technology systems and related processes must be improved in order to ensure timely and accurate determinations with respect to those who wish to enter our country and those who wish to apply for benefits under our immigrations laws. The management restructuring of the INS is on its way—a mandate the President and the Congress have given me—and the improvement of our information technology systems is moving ahead and can be accomplished with the help and support of Congress.

Mr. Chairman, I would like to say one word about INS employees and the events of September 11. Within hours of the attacks, the INS was working closely with the FBI to help determine who perpetrated these crimes and to bring those people to justice. Within 24 hours, under "Operation Safe Passage," The INS deployed several hundred Border Patrol agents to eight major U.S. airports to increase security, prevent further terrorist incidents and restore a sense of trust to the traveling public. At America's ports of entry, INS inspectors continue to work tirelessly to inspect arriving visitors, while ensuring the flow of legitimate commerce and tourism. Meanwhile, despite the tragedies and the disruptions, our service operations have managed to complete over 35,000 naturalizations nationwide and process thousands of other applications since September 11. America should be proud of the extraordinary effort of these men and women.

Looking Ahead

It has been said that after September 11 "everything has changed." I hope that is not true. America must remain America, a symbol of freedom and a beacon of hope to those who seek a better life for themselves and their children. We must increase our security and improve our systems but in doing so we must not forget what has made this nation great—our openness to new ideas and new people, and a commitment to individual freedom, shared values, innovation and the free market. If, in response to the events of September 11, we engage in excess and shut out what has made America great, then we will have given the terrorists a far greater victory than they could have hoped to achieve.

Thank you for this opportunity to appear, Mr. Chairman. I look forward to your questions.

Chairman KENNEDY. Thank you very much, Mr. Ziglar, for your very comprehensive testimony.

We have a very important and interesting panel that will be following this panel, so we will use 7-minute rounds in this time.

Mr. Ziglar, the media has reported that hundreds of foreign nationals have been detained by the INS and FBI since the morning of September 11th, and many are suspected of having ties to Al Qaeda or other terrorist organizations. Others are described as material witnesses. But the category includes people who may have been neighbors of the hijackers or have other possible associations that may well be innocent.

What can you tell us about the cautions the INS and Department of Justice are taking to ensure that the basic rights of innocent persons swept up in the early stages of the investigation are being adequately protected?

Mr. ZIGLAR. Mr. Chairman, we have been—let me back into the answer. We have been releasing a number of people based upon the information provided us by the FBI and based upon investigations and that sort of thing. And the number of people that we have in detention roughly is about 146, I think as we speak today, and that has, of course, come down from the numbers that you may have seen in the past.

That is the INS custody. I can't speak for the warrants and the other part of the process which we are not involved in.

We have a process that we have to charge somebody within 48 hours, and so that we have given notice to the court that we have someone and we charge them, and they are then entitled to a bond hearing. Those people that have gone forward on bond hearings, in some cases it has been continued. In some cases, judges have allowed us to continue to detain people.

There are reasons for detention of somebody who is out of status. You have to remember that these people, all these people, are out of status. They are not here legally at the moment.

One of the reasons for continuing detention is to—

Chairman KENNEDY. All the people, then, that the INS has detained are not here legally?

Mr. ZIGLAR. To my knowledge, everyone is out of status. If that is not true, I will let you know, but that is my knowledge.

One of the issues, of course, in whether you detain somebody is whether there is a flight risk, and way before September 11th, flight risk was always a big problem if you had somebody out of status and they were trying to stay here. So that is one of the grounds for staying. If they are a potential harm to the community, that is another ground. Obviously if they are aggravated felons under the 1996 Act, that is yet another ground.

Mr. Chairman, you know about me. I am big on due process and I am big on civil liberties and that sort of things. And certainly under my administration here, I am doing my best to make sure that people's civil liberties are not violated and, more importantly, that the process is honored, even though we have a crisis on our hands.

To my knowledge, we are going through the process, and we are keeping people in the process from the INS perspective. I can't talk about the rest of what is going on elsewhere because I don't know.

Chairman KENNEDY. So your answer, as I understand it, is that they are out of status, that they are here illegally, and that you are following the same kinds of procedures with regards to them that were in place prior to September 11th.

Mr. ZIGLAR. Absolutely.

Chairman KENNEDY. Let me come back to Mary Ryan. In the time I have available, there are a number of items, so I will try and ask the questions quickly, and if we get the response as well.

I am interested in your reaction to the development of a consular corps. I think many of us have known that those that have been in the area of that responsibility have been wonderfully dedicated people, in many instances younger members of the corps. It is a very, very tough, demanding job, and it is not one that has offered great opportunities for career advancement and otherwise. And one of the suggestions from one of our colleagues that has been thought about, Senator Bob Graham of Florida talked about the development of a consular corps that would not be greatly dissimilar from the Corps of Engineers in the military. It is a separate career, and there is a lot of professionalism, and there is a good deal of satisfaction developed through there, and esprit as well.

I wanted to get your reaction.

Ms. RYAN. Senator, I would argue with you that that is probably not the best way to go. I think what we have now in the Foreign Service is a generalist corps. We have four specializations, one of which is consular, and the people who are doing that work are proud of being Foreign Service officers and proud of being consular cone officers.

I think that if you went to a consular corps, in fact, you would even further limit career opportunities for those people in the corps. Right now we are getting more—not quite yet our share, I would argue, but more of the opportunities to serve as ambassadors and as assistant Secretaries, as deputy chiefs of mission, and as principal officers. And I think to take us out of the State Department and the Foreign Service and put us into another area would limit those opportunities considerably. You would not be able to hope for an ambassadorial assignment if you were in the consular corps separate from the State Department and separate from the Foreign Service.

I hear a lot of talk about how our newer officers, our younger officers don't like the work, and I am sure that that is one of the concerns that you have and others have. But I would say to you, Senator, that they do the work with dedication and commitment. And they are proud to do the work. They are patriots. We don't talk about Government employees very much anymore as patriots, and I think we have to start talking about it again.

It has been a long time since President Kennedy challenged my generation about the nobility of public service, and still we get really talented, really wonderful people to come into our Government and to come into the Foreign Service, into the civil service. And they don't come for the money. As you well know, the salaries are very low, and particularly at the lower grades, and a lot of these people have very big student loans to repay. And they don't come for prestige because, frankly, Senator, Mr. Chairman, there is no more prestige in serving in the Government, unfortunately. It has been a long time since anybody talked about public service and the need to serve our country and give something back to our country, which has nurtured us and supported us and protected us. And I hope that out of this tragedy of September 11th we start hearing more call for people to join the Government and join in the fight against terrorism.

Chairman KENNEDY. Well, I think that is a wonderful expression, and I think you deserve great credit, 35 years in the service of our country. We have had a good opportunity to work with you over a long period of that time. I personally have high regard for you and for the work that you have done.

The real question is how we get support for the consular corps, obviously in intelligence, which you have raised, and all the rest. But this is an issue about how we can make sure, in this process to use all our assets—our experience, the best in technology, and our intelligence. Out of that 550 million, we are talking about those handful of people that are out there, and we want and need the best in terms of technology to be able to use intelligence and experience to protect our nation. And we need to examine all of these issues to do that. But I appreciate your references.

My time is up, but I am still going to ask the question. On the time for adopting the machine-readable passports, I want to get your answer quickly on that. Then I had a question for Mr. Ziglar, we collect resources to be able to use from the fees of immigrants, and we are using those fees for our new technology. Is that the way we want to try and fund it? With the challenge that we are facing now, should we depend upon those fees to be able to bring your agency up to the kind of full speed ahead in terms of the newer technologies? I would just ask those two questions. I will hear from Mary Ryan first.

Ms. RYAN. Senator, on the first question about machine-readable passports, I think you mean in connection with the visa waiver program. Is that right, sir?

Chairman KENNEDY. Yes.

Ms. RYAN. Every country that is in the visa waiver program has a machine-readable passport now, except for Switzerland, which is going to introduce the machine-readable passport in 2003. But all the others have machine-readable passports, and they are issuing them now to their citizens.

The other question on visa fees, Mr. Chairman, I am enormously grateful to the Congress for giving us the authorization in fiscal year 1994 to charge a fee and to keep the money, because that has made all the difference in how we are able to do our work, a tremendous boost for us in consular operations.

We would have collapsed in the 1990s without that money, and this is money that the alien pays to apply for a non-immigrant visa. So all the money—and it is now a fortune; it is about $400 million a year—comes from aliens paying for the privilege of applying for a visa. And that means no taxpayer money has been used for our improvements. And we have automated the world. We are online. Every visa post has online connectivity to our CLASS database in real-time. And we can get instant information from it. As long as the information is in there, we can provide the consular officer in the field, no matter where he or she is, with this information instantly. And it is thanks to the wisdom of the Congress in giving us this authorization to charge and keep this money and our ability to spend it wisely.

Chairman KENNEDY. You don't want to talk about it too much because someone will try and get their hands on it.

[Laughter.]

Mr. ZIGLAR. Mr. Chairman, I am really glad you asked that question, and I can talk about it for a long time, but the answer is that if we want to develop our technology base, whether it is the SEVIS system or anything else, we simply have got to have the money up front to do it. Paying it on a pay-as-you-go basis, a revenue-as-you-go basis is very, very difficult because, as you know, you have got to have the money in the bank before you can commit under the Federal rules.

So if we don't have the money, we can't commit, and that means that we drag these projects out over a very long time. Appropriated money up front and preferably no-year money so that we can make these commitments beyond one year would be extremely helpful to expediting the process. And even if you want us to pay it back, I mean, make us a loan, but we need the money to get going.

Chairman KENNEDY. Very good. Thank you.

Senator Brownback?

Senator BROWNBACK. Thank you, Mr. Chairman. I find so many statements here that I agree with and a lot of questions that I have at the same time.

I want to thank you for your comments, Ms. Ryan, about the nobility of public service. I met with my staff this morning and mentioned to them that the terrorism war on the United States, if I could put it that way, has been going on for 10 years and the front line has been our diplomatic corps and our men and women overseas. And on September 11th it reached our shores, and right now the front line is the Hart Office Building and in places here that it is taking place. There is a true beauty and nobility of that service, and I appreciate your mentioning that.

I also want to say to Mr. Ziglar, I appreciate his comments about the problem here, and not to cast all immigrants into this stew, we had a few people, non-immigrant visas that were issued here, that sought to do us harm and, unfortunately, accomplished that. But let's not compromise our values or our economy in a process of dealing with this. So that is why the issue becomes, I guess, far trickier and more difficult to hone in on.

But that is what I want to try to do, and that is what we are working on in the legislation that we have here. And I would invite all of your input to us, as we try to craft this and get this out in a quick fashion, as to what is it that we need to do and what we need to be putting forward.

On a primary note, first and foremost, you talk about information sharing and the stovepipes that are currently in place. Are each of you confident that we are getting those stovepipes broken down and the information being shared in a timely fashion? And if not, what are the problems?

Mr. ZIGLAR. Senator, I would have to say this: You have got to remember, I haven't been down there but 2 months. I did have a month's experience before all of this happened. It was clear to me that there was a lot of information holding and not sharing among a lot of agencies. That has gotten a whole lot better since September the 11th on what I would have to regard as a patchwork basis, and Mary can certainly speak for herself as to how she feels about it.

I think there is a slow but inevitable cultural change going on that says that we can't have this happen again, and if sharing of information—or lack of sharing of information was one of the problems, we have got to get over it and quit playing bureaucratic games with information.

I think we are getting there, but I think there is a long way to go. Certainly at the ports of entry and at the consular offices around the world, we need a lot more information from intelligence agencies and law enforcement agencies that we can access on a real-time basis to determine whether the person standing in front of us is somebody who should not be here, is inadmissible to the United States.

I think Ambassador Ryan certainly made that point in her testimony. I couldn't endorse what she said more strongly.

Senator BROWNBACK. Ambassador Ryan, are the stovepipes being broke down?

Ms. RYAN. I hope that the Commissioner is right about the stovepipes are being broken down. I am not completely confident that they are. I think that there is still a very great concern among the intelligence and law enforcement agencies about protection of sources and methods, which I would think after September 11th has to give way to concern for protection of lives.

We are the front lines. The consular officer overseas is the front line of defense of this Nation. We are the outer ring of border security, and we have been trying, for example, for quite a long time to get FBI NCIC III access. And we were denied over and over again because we are not a law enforcement agency. I think that has to change. I think there has to be a recognition that we are on the front lines, that we have a responsibility to protect our Nation just as they do, and that they have to give us the information. I don't really care how they do it or what sort of code system they want to use to protect the information, but they have to give us the information.

Senator BROWNBACK. Did we know about these gentlemen that were involved in the terrorist activities from some of our intelligence community information that wasn't shared with State or INS?

Ms. RYAN. Senator, I don't know that. What I do know is that we had no information whatsoever on those 19. I don't know whether—

Senator BROWNBACK. The State Department did not.

Ms. RYAN. The State Department had no information. In our CLASS lookout—

Senator BROWNBACK. Do we have it in other places in the Government—

Ms. RYAN. —we had nothing on them. I don't know whether that means there was no information or whether the information was not shared with us. I just know we had nothing on any of the 19.

Senator BROWNBACK. Mr. Ziglar?

Mr. ZIGLAR. The same is true with us. Now, whether there was other information someplace else, I don't know the answer to that either, like Ambassador Ryan. But we didn't.

Senator BROWNBACK. It seems like that is something that—

Chairman KENNEDY. If the Senator would yield, does the Central Intelligence Agency give you names of terrorists?

Ms. RYAN. The Intelligence Agency does give us names through the Visas Viper program and through TIPOFF, which is run by our intelligence and research bureau. And, in fact, they have given us thousands of names over the years, since we set up that program. But they don't give us—in my opinion, we do not get all the information.

Senator BROWNBACK. Well, if I could interrupt you as well, as I understand, Ambassador Ryan, they give you information but it is on a haphazard basis. It is not necessarily a timely basis. You may get it a month or 2 months after it is acquired. And so there is no system, and it really is a patchwork and almost kind of a "who do you know" type of system that has been in place. Is that correct?

Ms. RYAN. It is not as effective as I think it should be. For example, on a couple of the terrorists, we were given names in August and asked to revoke visas. And when we looked at what they gave us, we had no information on one, one had been refused a visa, and two had been issued. One visa had already expired. And that was in August.

I don't know when they had that information. I don't know when they got that information. But you do wonder, if they knew it in August, when they might have known it earlier than August.

Senator BROWNBACK. My point in this—and I am sensing your frustration, having been around this for some period of time—is that with the front line of the war on terrorism being on our shores here, in New York City and Washington and Nevada, in places all across this country, the issue of protection of sources and methods within the intelligence community, which I fully support and I think is appropriate, but we have got to be able to design some system that, if the terrorist is the person that tries to move in amongst us and blow themselves up along with a number of us at the same time, then we have got to try and find that needle and have all the information absolutely available.

Mr. Ziglar's point about we have 350 million entrants, non–U.S. citizens, across our border every year and that we are looking for a dozen, 50, something like that, seeking to do us harm, that is more than the proverbial needle in a haystack. And so the information sharing that we have to have is probably the most critical component of our protection of ourselves in this war on terrorism.

Mr. ZIGLAR. Senator, let me make one point. There is no silver bullet. A lot of these folks that were involved in this thing were young, had no records; there was no intelligence to gather on them. They had been recruited at very young ages. They had never been in trouble. So there may never be any information on them because there is no information to gather. So you are faced with a faceless enemy sometimes.

Now, obviously there are other situations where you may be able to gather information about people. So it is not a silver bullet. If we shared every piece of information we had with every Government agency everywhere, we might still not be able to detect everybody who intends to come here and do harm to us.

Senator BROWNBACK. But we could do a lot better.

Mr. ZIGLAR. We can do a lot better, absolutely, and we need to. But I just want to make sure that people don't think that there is a silver bullet that will absolutely protect us.

Senator BROWNBACK. I think I am more looking for a magnet for that needle in the haystack.

A couple quick comments, and then I will pass along. One is on this biometrics system for people coming into the country, which I think is very important and I hope we can speed its implementation. You gave some time lines on that which I might want to discuss with you.

We just had the Deputy Prime Minister of Canada in, and we were talking about standardizing how we would do the biometrics testing, because apparently different countries are looking at different ways, in particular as we look at a North American perimeter in all probability, that we need to be working closely with the Canadians and Mexicans, the Mexican Government, at least on establishing that standardization and doing so in a quick fashion.

I applaud your looking at the number of schools that can authorize student visas and their standard reviews. At Pittsburg State University in my State of Kansas over the weekend, the President was talking about the international students there, a wonderful gift to the school, really, because it really helps them and it is a diverse population that they really like. But then also I hear of stories of other places, and I am really questioning that. So I am glad you are looking into that.

Finally, God bless you all. This is a tough task, but you are all up to it, and I really appreciate your coming forth here. You help inspire confidence in us, and I think in the people, that we are on top of this and we are hardening our targets here at home at the front line, the programs we are doing of who gets into the United States, and yet still not compromising our values or our economy.

Ms. RYAN. Thank you, Senator.

Chairman KENNEDY. Senator Grassley?

Senator GRASSLEY. Yes, thank you very much.

This talk about a silver bullet—and I don't disagree with what Mr. Ziglar said, but it reminds me of a certain lethargy we have in Government of willingness to share information. And I think the terrorist attack just surfaced a problem that permeates Government over a long period of time, that somehow, you know, the CIA or any agency this could apply to, but the CIA, it is our work and we have got certain information. It is almost like we have got a proprietary right to it, and some other agency has got their work and their proprietary interest in it. And instead of having an attitude we ought to have—and I think we are getting this attitude now along the lines of what Ms. Ryan says, that there is an attitude of cooperation and patriotism and public service, that this isn't this agency's work and our property and this agency's property, but it is the property of the American people, and we are all in this boat together. And under the circumstances we are in right now, we might sink or swim together. So I guess we have got to change the bureaucratic attitude that has been there for a long period of time.

Along this line, I want to ask my first question of Mr. Ziglar, and I go back to your confirmation hearing. I asked about the information sharing between the Immigration Service and the Internal Revenue Service. I was told that your agency does not verify tax information from immigrants with the IRS, particularly the matter of whether the immigrants are paying taxes. The INS needs to work with the IRS, I believe, in regard to immigrants who come to this country on work visas. The INS should work with the IRS to verify an immigrant is actually working. If the immigrant on a work visa is not working, the INS needs to have him tracked down, just like we track down foreign students who don't show up at their designated school.

The Internal Revenue Service has certain data that can be extremely useful to all law enforcement, particularly the INS, in its efforts to track down violators. So I am asking you today to make sure that the appropriate information from the IRS is being pursued by the INS. No one knows if any of this would have stopped the attacks of September the 11th. They are obviously not a silver bullet. But we need to make sure that we work to prevent terrorism with every weapon that we have.

So I would like to know whether you agree with me on this matter and what you can do with the IRS information to better make use of it and what limitations there are that might prevent you from getting the IRS information you need, assuming that you don't have to change law—or maybe you do have to change law.

Mr. ZIGLAR. Well, Senator, I couldn't agree with you more that the exchange of information and that particular kind of information could very well be very valuable in a law enforcement or immigration law enforcement context.

At the time of my confirmation hearing, you and I know Senator Kennedy and a number of other members of the Committee asked me to look into a number of things, which I was doing during the course of my first month there, and September 11th came along and I have not focused on some of those questions. But I can tell you this: In terms of this investigation, I have noted the presence of the Treasury Department, the IRS in that context. And it is something that I believe that going forward, certainly from our perspective, will be valuable information for us to know, particularly as hopefully we ramp up our efforts to identify those people who are overstaying their visas, for example,, or overstaying their welcome, if you will, and identifying them and using that potentially as a way of—I hate to use the words "tracking them down," but tracking them down.

Senator GRASSLEY. Would you be able to maybe look into my specific questions and then give me an answer in writing, maybe in 5 days? Would that be—

Mr. ZIGLAR. Yes, I will do my best, sir.

Senator GRASSLEY. Thank you.

Also, in your testimony before the House Subcommittee on Immigration, you mentioned the database system called ENFORCE, which draws on other databases that the INS has. Could you give us more detail about that technology and if the database would improve data sharing within the agency?

Mr. ZIGLAR. I would be happy to talk to you about that because I am excited about what we are doing. ENFORCE is, for lack of a better technical terms, is a consolidating program, a consolidating database that draws from the many databases we have in the enforcement side of the INS. But, more importantly, or as importantly, it also has the capacity to reach out and access the databases of other Government agencies. For example, we could reach out and get data from the Department of State and bring it into our system so that we have one place where we can go and find out information about whoever it is.

That system, the ENFORCE system, which is, you know, cutting-edge from our point of view, it is trying to deal with the stovepipe effect of having all this information in one—getting it in one place instead of having it in a hundred different places. It has also been integrated with our IDENT system. Now, the IDENT system is one that—it is a fingerprint system, a biometric system, and as we pick up people or in certain circumstances we get their fingerprints, it goes into this electronic database. Somebody can show up in front of us. We put their fingers into this reader. It tells us who they are. That doesn't necessarily tell us anything about them.

We then go to ENFORCE through this same system, and that gathers the information from all of our databases as well as reaching outside.

Now, is it fully functional yet? No, it is not. We are taking our different stovepipe modules, if you will, and integrating them into ENFORCE as we speak. We were doing that before September the 11th. This is not something that we are hurrying up and trying to get done as a result of September 11th. It is something the INS was doing before.

And if I could just make one point, I know the INS has taken a lot of heat for a lot of things and a lot of criticism, and a lot of it has been justified, and the people there will tell you it has been justified. But an awful lot of real progress has been made at that organization to address the technology, to address the information issue, to address the management issues there. And I found the organization a much better organization than was painted to me as I was going through the confirmation and the people there are very dedicated. They want to do the right thing, and they have done the right thing, in my view, certainly since September 11th. They have performed superbly, magnificently.

Senator GRASSLEY. Thank you, Mr. Chairman.

Chairman KENNEDY. Thank you. Thank you very much.

We appreciate all of your testimony and responses to questions. We will be continuing. We look forward to working with you.

Mr. ZIGLAR. Thank you.

Ms. RYAN. Thank you.

Mr. GUTIERREZ. Thank you, Mr. Chairman.

Chairman KENNEDY. It is a privilege to introduce our second panel: Jeanne Butterfield, executive director, American Immigration Lawyers Association, an American immigration law foundation; Demetrios Papademetriou, who is co-director and co-founder of the Migration Policy Institute; and Richard Norton, who is executive director of the International Biometric Industry Association.

Jeanne Butterfield has been a strong advocate for fair and efficient immigration laws for many years. Before joining the American Immigration Lawyers, she served as legal director of Centro Presente, a Central American refugee center in Boston, and worked in private immigration law practice. She is an expert in a wide range of immigration challenges, including family- and employment-based immigration issues, and refugee and asylum issues. She has extensive experience working with government agencies to ensure the fair and effective implementation of our immigration laws and regulations.

Dr. Papademetriou helped establish the Migration Policy Institute. Before that, he was a Senior Associate at the Carnegie Endowment for International Peace, where he directed the International Migration Policy Program. He has impressive experience dealing with North American border issues, migration management, and many other major immigrant issues. He recently co-authored a book entitled, "*Caught in the Middle: Border Communities in an Era of Globalization*." In addition the Migration Policy Institute has recently published an extensive paper called "Immigration and National Security" discussing immigration reforms in light of the terrorist attacks.

Richard Norton founded the International Biometric Industry Association in 1998 to represent the interests industry manufacturers in the use of biometric technology; executive vice president of Identification Technology Partners; previously a consultant on border control technology, served 19 years at the Immigration and Naturalization Service, been a leader on border control for many years, advising airlines, airports, governments, and technology providers on biometric technologies.

I thank all of you for being here. Ms. Butterfield, we look forward to your testimony.

STATEMENT OF JEANNE A. BUTTERFIELD, EXECUTIVE DIRECTOR, AMERICAN IMMIGRATION LAWYERS ASSOCIATION, WASHINGTON, D.C.

Ms. BUTTERFIELD. Thank you very much, Mr. Chairman, and distinguished members of the Subcommittee. I really appreciate this opportunity to present my views on current U.S. immigration policy, and I hope that my written testimony provides some useful perspectives on how we can develop—

Chairman KENNEDY. We will include all of the testimony. The written testimony will be made a part of the record.

Ms. BUTTERFIELD. All right. Thank you. To develop immigration controls that are effective in deterring terrorism and enhancing our Nation's security. We need to undertake these reforms to our immigration system with a very fundamental understanding, which I know you all share: that we are a Nation of immigrants, that immigration remains central to who we are as a country and helps explain our success as a people and a Nation. We have to take on this task as well with the clear understanding that it is precisely in times of danger that we must fiercely defend our Constitution and the protections and liberties that distinguish us from other nations.

My testimony overviews some of the current measures and powers that the INS and Department of State already have that can be used more effectively, I believe, if properly coordinated with good intelligence information to deter terrorism. And you have heard about that already this morning.

I will also include here some proposals about new measures that Congress could and should consider that would add perhaps to our deterrence capabilities. So let me just touch on briefly to remind us what our current powers and procedures are that really don't require enhancement in terms of new laws, but perhaps require more effective integration with intelligence data.

Current immigration law provides the Government with extraordinary powers to deny admission to any person who we believe might be intending to come to the United States to violate our laws and endanger our safety. You have heard from Ms. Ryan earlier that consular officers, as you know, around the world have virtually unreviewable discretion to deny a visa to any person for any number of reasons listed in our statutes. And I enumerate those in my written testimony. But let me just call one to your attention.

A person who a consular officer or the INS has reasonable grounds to believe seeks to enter the United States to engage even incidentally in any unlawful activity is simply inadmissible. So I think we have the tools in our statutes. The question is how do we apply them and how do we make those determinations. And I know you are being very thoughtful about the many thorny questions that poses.

Unfortunately, our laws are only as good as the information available to those who are enforcing our laws, and we have yet to devise a system that will allow a consular officer in an overseas post to gaze into a person's heart or mind and somehow divine their intentions. Stricter scrutiny I think can deter the casual criminal, but it is unlikely to deter those who have no known criminal record, no evidence of association with any known terrorist organization or activity, and yet whose heart is intent on committing a heinous crime amongst us, sometimes years hence.

We have in our laws, secondly, extensively grounds of deportability which give the Government the power to deport anyone who has engaged in any terrorist activity, including planning, material support, harboring, and all of these grounds are listed, again, in my written testimony.

Again, in this instance, the Government has the full power to deport anyone who presents a danger here on terrorism grounds, but deportation, as we know, is no deterrence for those who fully intend to end their lives while committing a heinous terrorist act.

The third set of powers that we currently have which you talked earlier with Mr. Ziglar about are the detention powers. We currently have the powers at our disposal to detain someone pending and continuing through their deportation hearing and any subsequent appeal. And it is those existing powers which have allowed the INS to detain, as Mr. Ziglar said this morning, I think currently some 146 persons on suspected immigration violations. And those powers are also being contemplated to be expanded in the legislation that the Senate enacted last week, which would give the Attorney General new power to certify someone as a suspected terrorist or somehow involved in terrorist activity, and would trigger a mandatory detention power.

I appreciate the work that you, Senators, and your staffs have done to really ensure that these new powers, when enacted, will not be abused and that there will be some safeguards and court review and protections to make sure that detention is necessary to protect national security and does not go on indefinitely.

I would just remind us all in passing—and, again, more elaborated in my written testimony—that we also have at our disposal the Alien Terrorist Removal Court, an extraordinary set of justices put together to hear secret evidence cases that was created in our 1996 law, which has not yet been convened or used, but that is at the Government's disposal should they need it.

We have expedited removal, which allows the INS o turn people back right at the port of entry, and screen people, again, it is the second point of review, really, after the consular visa issuance decision where, again people are subject to all the grounds of inadmissibility and can be put through an expedited hearing.

We have extensive reporting requirements. You have already talked about the SEVIS system for student reporting and the current procedures in place to verify departures, so I will not elaborate on those.

Let me turn just briefly to other new measures that we should be considering, some of which you have already heard about. I want to add my voice to those of Mr. Ziglar and others who say, first and foremost, with all of these measures, we need increased funding for the INS and the Department of State. In order to effectively fight terrorism by enhancing our intelligence capabilities, DOS and INS need to upgrade their technological infrastructures. These new databases we are talking about and all of the real-time shared information are not inexpensive, and I don't believe that that funding can come strictly from user fees. I think it needs direct Federal appropriations, and I urge the Senate to address that concern.

There are several new technologies that are very promising, and I know that you heard about some of them, the face recognition from Ms. Ryan earlier today, the lookout lists and the need to integrate and make all of the Federal law enforcement agency and intelligence agency lists available one to the other. And I will not elaborate there.

Pre-inspection I think is one area that perhaps hasn't been touched on and I would urge you all to consider expanding. We do have pre-inspection at foreign airports currently in five countries in the world, and this is a procedure that allows a more calm and considered, perhaps, review of a person's admissibility before they even board an airplane. I think that program is a really useful one and could be expanded in several places in the world and would be very promising in creating some of those layers of security, perimeter layers, starting with the U.S. consuls abroad, then pre-inspection at the foreign airports, then the transmittal of the passenger list that Mr. Ziglar talked about; and finally, upon arrival in North America, increased cooperation amongst North American nations to create this kind of perimeter safety zone. And I know my colleague Demetri is going to address that further.

I want to conclude with just two concerns as we consider all of this, including the exit/entry control system. I know that the Senate heard testimony a couple of years ago about the exit/entry control system at the land borders, and I want to just urge your review of that information that was provided at the time.

I am from Michigan originally, and the Ambassador Bridge in Detroit is one that I have crossed many times. And in that testimony that you all heard some years ago, many experts pointed out that the Ambassador Bridge has 30,000 vehicle passings every day. And if we could design a very efficient and fast system and could determine that only half of those vehicles needed to be entered into our exit/entry control system and that process only took 30 seconds, you would have basically 4 or 5 days of backlog traffic simply to implement that system at that one land border. And I think that addresses the concern that Mr. Brownback shared earlier about we can't take measures that are going to undermine our economy and hurt our cross-border commerce. And that is a very real concern here.

The final two points. In all of these measures, we have to be mindful of the continued needs of asylum seekers and our international and domestic obligations to afford protection to those fleeing persecution. Pre-inspection at foreign airports is well and good, but in that process we are going to need to provide trained asylum officers so that those seeking our protection are not merely excluded somewhere overseas where we never then hear about them. There is a challenge there, I think, that is a very real one that we need to take to heart.

Finally, all of this data collection and recordkeeping is only as useful as the correlation with good intelligence information. I think we keep coming back full circle to intelligence. If we were able to document the entry and exit of all of the 30 million non-immigrants who come in and out each year to this country, and that created some big giant database. What would that tell us? Would that tell us that the person who overstayed their visa for a week or two weeks or even a month did so to spend an extra week at Disney World, or because Grandma had a sinus infection and couldn't fly on the airplane, or for some other purely innocent reason? Or does it tell us that the person overstayed and is intending somehow to commit a heinous crime amongst us? That is where all of the data collection in the world is not going to make us any more secure or safe unless we find a way efficiently and in a focused manner to correlate it with good intelligence, intelligence, intelligence.

As the current situation calls out for change in the direction of more effective means of deterring terrorism, we can't lost sight of these fundamental values of this Nation of immigrants. As we seek to create new means to isolate terrorists, we must take care not to isolate America in the process.

Thank you.

[The prepared statement of Ms. Butterfield follows:]

STATEMENT OF JEANNE A. BUTTERFIELD, AMERICAN IMMIGRATION LAWYERS ASSOCIATION

Mr. Chairman and Distinguished Members of the Subcommittee:

My name is Jeanne A. Butterfield and I am the Executive Director of the American Immigration Lawyers Association (AILA). I appear today as an observer and participant in the development of U.S. immigration policy for nearly twenty years, eight of those years with AILA. AILA is the national bar association of nearly 8,000 attorneys and law professors who represent the entire spectrum of applicants for immigration adjudications.

I appreciate this opportunity to present our views on current U.S. immigration policy and I hope to provide some useful perspectives on how we can develop immigration controls that are effective in deterring terrorism and enhancing our nation's security. We need to undertake this task on several fronts, with immigration reform being one important aspect of the effort. As we develop reforms in this area, we need to make sure that they are effective. We cannot allow false solutions to real problems to lull us into a degree of security we have not achieved.

We need to undertake reforms to our immigration system with this important understanding: that we are a nation of immigrants, that immigration remains central to who we are as a country and helps explain our success as a people and a nation. Furthermore, we must take on this task with the clear understanding that it is precisely in times of danger that we must fiercely defend our Constitution and the protections and liberties that distinguish us from other nations.

We must recognize that existing laws and procedures offer us significant protections and pose certain problems. I thus will begin with an overview of current measures and powers that the Immigration and Naturalization Service and Department of State already have that can be used more effectively, if properly coordinated with good intelligence information, to deter terrorism. I will conclude with some proposals about new measures that Congress could mandate that would add to our deterrence capabilities.

CURRENT POWERS AND PROCEDURES

1. GROUNDS OF INADMISSIBILITY

Current immigration law provides the government with extraordinary powers to deny admission to any person we believe might be intending to come to the United States to violate our laws and endanger our safety.

Consular officers in posts around the world have virtually unreviewable discretion to deny a visa to any person for any number of reasons listed in our statutes. Further, as a second layer of deterrence and protection, anyone who is issued a visa abroad is subject a second time to these same grounds of inadmissibility when they present themselves to an INS inspector for inspection and entry at any U.S. port of entry (airport or land border). A person can be denied admission on either of these two occasions denied a visa in the first instance, or denied entry in the second.

The Immigration and Nationality Act (INA) provides several broad national security-related grounds upon which any person can be denied a visa to enter the United States:

a) a person who a consular officer or INS has "reasonable ground to believe" seeks to enter the U.S. to engage, even incidentally, in any unlawful activity is inadmissible (INA Section 212(a)(3)(A)(ii));

b) a person who has engaged in terrorist activity is inadmissible (INA Section 212(a)(3)(B)(i)(I)); terrorist activity is broadly defined and includes, among the more commonly identified activities such as hijackings, the following range of activities (INA Section 212(a)(3)(B)(ii) and (iii))

1) the use of any firearm with the intent to endanger the safety of even one individual;
2) the solicitation of funds for terrorist activity or terrorist organization;
3) the solicitation for membership to engage in terrorist activity or in an terrorist organization;
4) the provision of any type of material support for terrorist activity or for any person who plans to commit a terrorist activity;
5) the gathering of information on potential targets, or any preparation or planning of a terrorist activity;

c) a person who a consular officer or INS has "reasonable ground to believe" is likely to engage after entry in any terrorist activity is inadmissible (INA Section 212(a)(3)(B)(i)(II));

d) a person whose entry or activities in the U.S. the Secretary of State has reasonable ground to believe would have potentially serious adverse foreign policy consequences for the United States is inadmissible (INA Section 212(a)(C)).

These extensive grounds of inadmissibility make it clear that the United States has extensive power and grounds to deny a visa or entry to anyone it has reason to believe may endanger the national security. The question properly before the INS, Department of State and U.S. Congress is how the various agencies that implement and enforce these laws can be provided with the necessary and timely intelligence information they need to properly apply these grounds of inadmissibility and prevent those who intend to commit terrorist acts from entering the country.

Unfortunately, our immigration admissions and visa issuance systems and laws are only as good as the information available to those enforcing them. We have yet to devise a system that will allow a U.S. consular officer or an INS inspector to gaze into a person's heart or mind and divine their intentions. Stricter scrutiny may deter the casual criminal, but it is unlikely to deter those who have no known criminal record, no evidence of association with an terrorist activity or organization, yet whose heart is intent on committing a heinous crime some months or years hence.

2. GROUNDS OF DEPORTABILITY

Once in the United States, any temporary non-immigrant (visitors, students, temporary workers) or lawful permanent resident can be detained and deported if they engage in terrorist activity.

Again, the grounds for deportability are broad, and give the government the power to deport anyone who has engaged in terrorist activities, including all of the activities enumerated above: planning, fundraising, soliciting for membership, providing material support for an organization's terrorist activity (INA Section 237((a)(4)(B).

A person is also deportable if he has engaged in "any other criminal activity which endangers public safety or national security (INA Section 237(a)(4)(A)(ii)). This ground of deportability does not require any criminal conviction.

If the government only later learns that a person was involved overseas in a foreign terrorist organization, or had otherwise engaged in a terrorist activity, that person too is later deportable, on the grounds that he was "inadmissible at time of entry".

Finally, an immigration judge has the power to deny asylum or other relief from deportation to a person who is otherwise eligible for that relief, if the person represents a threat to national security. Specifically, the statute includes mandatory bars to asylum relief for:

(a) anyone who "there are reasonable grounds for regarding. . .as a danger to the security of the United States (INA Section 208(b)(2)(A)(iv)); or

(b) the alien is inadmissible or deportable under several of the terrorism-related grounds of inadmissibility or deportability (INA Section 208(b)(2)(A)(v)).

In short, the government currently has broad and sufficient powers to deport anyone who presents a danger to the United States on terrorism grounds. Of course, deportation is no deterrence for those who fully intend to end their lives while committing a terrorist act.

3. DETENTION POWERS

The INS currently has very broad powers to detain someone pending and continuing through their deportation hearing and any subsequent appeal. Under current law, immigrants charged with deportability for terrorist activity or certain violent crimes have been found ineligible to even apply for release from custody (INA Section 236(c). For those immigrants who have the right to seek release on bond before an immigration judge, that request can be, and is often, denied if the person is deemed to be a threat to national security, a danger to the community or otherwise present a risk of flight.

The current regulations, recently amended and republished as an interim final regulation in the Federal Register by Attorney General Ashcroft (8 CFR Part 287, amending Section 287.3(d), provide further that a person may be detained without a warrant of arrest under the authority contained in Section 287(a)(2) of the INA. Under the regulation, as currently in force, a determination about whether actual immigration violation charges will be brought against a person will be made within 48 hours of the arrest, except in the event of an emergency or other extraordinary circumstance in which case a determination will be made within an additional reasonable period of time, whether the alien will be continued in custody or released on bond or recognizance and whether a notice to appear and warrant of arrest as prescribed in 8 CFR parts 236 and 239 will be issued. " (emphasis added)

It is these already extraordinary powers of detention that have allowed the Attorney General to detain some reported 165 persons on suspected technical immigration violations in recent weeks, with no determination being made to date for many about whether they will in fact be charged or not. The question must be posed here: what is "an additional reasonable period of time" under the regulations? Is two weeks reasonable in current circumstances? Is five weeks unreasonable? Those being detained, the press, the advocacy community and the Congress surely deserve an answer to this question.

In new powers contemplated in the pending "USA" Act (S. 15 10), the Attorney General will be given the power to implement mandatory detention of anyone he "certifies" that he has reasonable grounds to believe fall within the definition of "terrorist" or "terrorist activity" as outlined above. This new power will prevent a person so "certified" from seeking release on bond, whether or not the person is charged with deportability based on terrorist grounds or is simply charged with a technical visa violation.

These broad new powers, when enacted, must be used carefully and not be used to detain individuals indefinitely without proving that their detention is necessary to protect national security or the public.

4. ALIEN TERRORIST REMOVAL COURT

Congress in 1996 created the new Alien Terrorist Removal Procedures (INA Section 501 through 507). These procedures were designed to allow the government to conduct deportation hearings with the use of secret evidence. While the new court was to be composed of 5 district court justices appointed by the Chief Justice of the U.S. Supreme Court, a single justice is empowered to consider classified information presented ex pane and in camera.

In recognition of the extraordinary nature of such proceedings, certain protections were provided, including the right to be informed of the nature of the charges and a "general account" of the basis for the charges (the secret evidence), and the right to be represented by assigned counsel at government expense. (INA Section 504(b) and (c).

To date, this new Alien Terrorist Removal Court has not been convened. The government has, however, used "secret evidence" in regular deportation hearings, primarily in the context of bond determinations and in opposing applications for discretionary relief, such as political asylum or adjustment of status. (See, for more details about past secret evidence cases, Akram, Susan, Scheherezade Meets Kafka: Two Dozen Sordid Tales of Ideological Exclusion, Georgetown Immigration Law Journal, Fall, 1999; 14 Geo. Immigr. L.J. 5 1)

The use of secret evidence is anathema to a democracy. Its use, in the rare instances where the government strongly believes it is necessary to protect the life of confidential sources, should be confined to proceedings in the "Alien Terrorist Removal Court". The law governing these special proceedings, in recognition of their extraordinary nature, at least mandates certain protections, such as appointed counsel, for the accused.

5. EXPEDITED REMOVAL

The 1996 Illegal Immigration Reform and Immigration Responsibility Act (IIRAIRA) also provides the government with extraordinary new powers at U.S. ports of entry to deny admission and summarily remove any person who the INS inspector believes is presenting fraudulent documents, including a facially valid visa if there is some reason to believe that the visa was obtained through fraud or misrepresentation, or if the person is believed to be attempting to enter the U.S. for a purpose inconsistent with the terms of the visa.

The new expedited removal provisions have been scrutinized extensively because they run the danger of sweeping into their orbit legitimate asylum seekers who are most likely to be fleeing their persecutors without having first obtained proper travel documents. We must be careful not 'to create a process that a terrorist with adequate funding, education and documents can penetrate, but which turns away legitimate asylum seekers who have no documents and who are too scared or traumatized by abuse to adequately make their claim at the border.

However, the expedited removal powers contained in our immigration statutes give INS inspectors sweeping and unreviewable power to deny entry to suspected terrorists and return them on the next flight out. A person so excluded cannot obtain a visa to enter the U.S. for at least five years.

Clearly such powers must be used carefully and with adequate protections. The hapless visitor with entirely legitimate business purposes who is returned on the next plane to Singapore and denied a visa for the next five years has little recourse. There must be a means to challenge such mistakes, and to obtain a waiver of the five-year ban. In previous times, such a person could request a hearing before an immigration judge and present evidence to prove that their intent was legitimate. No more, under the terms of the 1996 laws.

However sweeping and subject to abuse, these powers do provide another existing means to deter terrorists. But, as outlined above, these powers to deny admission and summarily exclude are only as effective as the intelligence information provided to the INS inspector at the port of entry. What we do not want to see as a result is thousands of legitimate visitors and even refugees being summarily excluded, while international criminals and terrorists, who have the means to purchase or otherwise obtain valid documents, slip through undetected. That unfortunately may be the result of these expanded powers.

6. REPORTING REQUIREMENTS:

The operation of current reporting requirements for foreign students and the arrival and departure of passengers both are areas needing significant improvements.

a. Student Reporting

More than 500,000 foreign students last year were enrolled in colleges and universities around the country. These students are a vital part of our higher education system. In California, the state with the greatest number of international students, just over 66,000 students from 19992000 brought $1.6 billion dollars into the state's economy. Foreign students have made enormous contributions in the advancement of technology and science, and graduates from American colleges and universities have gone on to lead nations and shape history.

We have long understood that the opportunity to study in this country comes with rules and responsibilities that affect both the students and the institutions. All foreign students must apply for a visa and must be able to prove that they are not inadmissible to the United States. Since at least 1985, colleges and universities approved to receive foreign students are required to gather and report information about foreign students to the Immigration and Naturalization Service.

This information includes the student's current address, date of commencement of studies, the student's written application for admission and other supporting documents the school uses to determine eligibility, the date and reason for termination of a student, and any academic disciplinary actions taken against the student due to any criminal convictions.

In the aftermath of the 1993 bombing of the World Trade Center, the INS created the Coordinated Interagency Partnership for Regulating International Students (CIPRIS) as a pilot program to provide for the electronic transfer of student information between institutions and the INS. In 1996, IIRAIRA mandated that INS fully implement the CIPRIS system by 2001. After 1996, the INS found that it could not address all the technical problems and asked Congress for an extension of 2001 deadline.

Although the program to provide for the electronic transfer of the information collected on foreign students has yet to be implemented, colleges and universities are still required to collect and report the data to INS, and an INS officer can request access to it at any time.

At intervals specified by the INS, but not more frequently than once a term or session, the Service's processing center is required to send each school a list of all foreign students who, according to Service records, are attending that school. A designated school official at the school must note on the list whether or not each student on the list is pursuing a full course of study and give the names and current addresses of all student visa holders not listed, attending the school and other information specified by the Service as necessary to identify the students and to determine their immigration status.

The designated school official must comply with the request, sign the list, state his or her title, and return the list to the Service's processing center within sixty days of the date of the request. Failure to follow any of the procedures and regulations will result in the withdrawal of the schools approval to receive non-immigrant students.

The INS is working with colleges and universities to develop this system electronically. The electronic system is only beginning to be implemented as an operational prototype with 21 educational institutions. The failure, if any, of the student tracking system is not the absence of laws, but the lack of resources. Congress needs to provide funding to get this system up and running and maintained in those schools authorized to enroll foreign students.

As the prototype is expanded, the INS needs to assess and report to Congress on the feasibility of this system, and whether it can improve the security of the U.S. relative to implementation costs, and do so in a way that does not intrude excessively on the privacy rights and civil liberties of students.

b. Verifying Departures

Requiring airlines and other passenger carriers to identify passengers' arrivals and departures has been a part of our laws for many years. Passenger carriers are required by law to deliver to the immigration officers at the port of arrival and departure a list or manifest of the persons on board such vessel or aircraft. According to the law, "such lists or manifests shall be prepared at such time, be in such form and shall contain such information as the Attorney General shall prescribe by regulation as being necessary for the identification of the persons transported and for the enforcement of the immigration laws. "

This language grants broad power to the Attorney General to decide when and how an airline identifies its passengers. The problems we now have with identifying who is coming and going from our shores are technological, not legal. In 1997, the Office of the Inspector General found that the principal INS record-keeping system for tracking nonimmigrant overstays, the Nonimmigrant Information System (NIIS), does not produce reliable data.

Normally, passengers arriving in the United States fill out an I–94 form and present it to the INS inspector upon arrival. The inspector collects the arrival portion of the form and returns the departure portion to the passenger. The arrival portion is sent to an INS contractor, who inputs the data into NIIS. When the person leaves the United States, the airlines are supposed to collect the departure portion of the I–94 form and provide it to the INS for input into NIIS. The data is then matched by MIS to identify nonimmigrant overstays.

The OIG report found that the MIS data is incomplete and unreliable due to missing departure records and errors in records processing. MIS does not contain departure records for a large number of aliens, most of whom the INS assumes have left the United States. The INS believes that many of these unrecorded departures result from airlines failing to collect departure forms, aliens departing through land borders, data entry errors, records being lost through electronic transmission or tape-loading problems, and the failure of the system to match arrival and departure records.

The question that Congress must ask, as it considers the possible expansion of procedures to verify departures, is what use can be made of the extraordinary amount of data that would be collected under such procedures. The U.S. admits over 30 million non-immigrant visitors per year. If data regarding departures shows that just five percent of these visitors fail to depart at the end of their authorized stay, that information still does not inherently make us safer as a nation, nor does it deter terrorism.

NEW DETERRANCE MEASURES

What do we need to further enhance our nation's security? Enhancing this country's intelligence capacity is key. Any changes that we make to our immigration policy will work to the degree that they interface with, and take advantage of, enhanced intelligence information. Any such reforms must meet our due process and civil liberties concerns and standards.

There is much Congress and the Administration can do. Needed reforms include increased funding for the DOS and INS, increased access to lookout lists, reforms at our consulates, the use of new technologies, direct government funding of these technologies, more pre-inspections abroad, mandated in-flight transmittal of passenger lists, the creation of a North American Perimeter Safety Zone, and a workable entry-exit control system. These measures will help us to increase the layers of protection that stand between us and any potential adversaries from abroad.

We need to remember that our best protection derives from keeping targeted people from entering the U.S. Such measures are more effective and easier to implement than measures that focus on persons after they enter the United States. In all cases, we need to make sure that we keep out people who want to do us harm, not those seeking to come to our country for the reasons that people have always come here, including reuniting with their families, working or escaping persecution. The following new measures to increase security and deterrence should be carefully considered:

1. INCREASED FUNDING FOR DOS AND INS

It is important to increase funding and data access for the Department of State (DOS) and the Immigration and Naturalization Service (INS). At present, both agencies' computer systems are technologically obsolete, with different offices often unable to share information with the other, and some offices, especially those overseas, not even having computer capacity. In order to effectively fight terrorism by enhancing our intelligence capabilities and improving our border security, both the DOS and the INS need increased funding to upgrade their technological infrastructures. Such funding needs to come from direct federal appropriations. INS and DOS increased technological capacities cannot be supported through user fees. This enhanced capacity to meet our security needs is a national function best supported through the federal government.

2. THE USE OF NEW TECHNOLOGIES

Given the complexities of gathering, sharing and making accessible a great range of information about individuals and their identities, it is critical to make use of existing and emerging technologies to achieve the most reliable means of verifying identity. Traditionally, fingerprinting has served this function. However, any standard based on fingerprinting has significant limitations that new technologies can overcome. Lookout systems and other data networks can be further improved by the use of new technologies that can match a unique identifying characteristic of an individual with a name. One of these new, unintrusive technologies is a face recognition system that uses cameras to scan a person's face and compare the picture with a database containing the photos of persons about whom the authorities are interested. The database for this technology would contain only the images of persons the authorities are looking for and is relatively inexpensive.

The federal government needs to fund the development and use of these new technologies and make sure the various federal agencies coordinate compatible efforts in this area.

3. ACCESS TO LOOKOUT LISTS

U.S. federal agencies, as well as international law enforcement officials, need direct access to the various lookout lists maintained by different agencies. These lookout lists include the names of people who should not be admitted to the U.S. or should be pulled aside for questioning should the authorities come into contact with them. Increased funding would allow the agencies to build up their technological capacities so that, for example, DOS and INS. would be able to directly access the FBI and other agencies' databases to review information that would help them determine whether someone should be allowed to enter the U.S. or be granted a positive response to an application or petition. Such direct access would enable law enforcement agencies to act immediately to identify those high-risk individuals who seek to enter the U.S. or receive other immigration benefits. These lists need to be integrated and accessible, with the information updated in a timely manner.

We also must include safeguards against potential abuse of this data that would limit the redissemination of such information, ensure the security and confidentiality of such information, protect privacy rights of individuals who are subject to such information, and establish procedures that determine who stays on and is removed from these lists. Such safeguards will become even more necessary as the lists increase in size and unfamiliar names from various regions of the world may be incorrectly keyed in. We must make every effort to ensure the accuracy of the names on the list so that the wrong individual is not targeted.

4. CONSULATE REFORMS

Our intelligence gathering can be further improved by changing some of the operations of our consulates. As noted above, consulate staff cannot do their job if they have neither the necessary intelligence information nor the technological capacity to access, upload, and download this intelligence information in a timely manner. In addition, we need to upgrade the status of the consulate officer who interviews an applicant to assess whether the applicant is allowed to enter the U.S. Currently, this function tends to be performed by more junior personnel with less experience. In the future, each post should be required to have a core of civil service specialists who would remain at certain posts or be rotated between posts to increase the level of experience of the person who is making the important decision about who is given a visa to come to the U.S.

Furthermore, this decision needs to be reviewable. In these times of heightened scrutiny such review is vital to ensure the integrity of the system. We should welcome such a review as part of the checks and balances that are central to our democracy and vital to our system of protections. We recommend providing any applicant for entry or a visa, in writing, the reason for the denial of entry and an avenue for review of any denial based on this information. In those cases where the adverse decision is affirmed, the applicant should be provided with a means of appeal to the U.S. District Court in the District of Columbia

5. PRE-INSPECTION

U.S. pre-inspection programs are in effect in only S countries in the world—Canada, Ireland, Bermuda, the Bahamas, and Aruba. In these locations, passengers are in effect "pre-inspected" for admission to the U.S. before ever boarding a plane—passports are checked and names are run against the lookout list. This pre-inspection process allows more time for inspection and increases the likelihood of a more thorough check.

This procedure would move our system from one that focuses on a person's point of entry into the U.S. to one that focuses on their point of origin. The INS and DOS together would need to recommend where such pre-inspections should take place, as it would be impossible to undertake this procedure at every airport in the world. It also would be important to deal with host countries about any sovereignty issues that might arise when someone is to be arrested, with U.S. officials working cooperatively with authorities at the pre-clearance site who have the power to arrest and detain. Such cooperation should include assurances that suspected terrorists are not released because the host country authorities do not view the threat as seriously as does the U.S.

Congress needs to carefully examine and weigh the costs of such a pre-inspection program. As with other programs to increase security and deterrence, the federal government will need to find ways to fund such initiatives. The cost of setting up and maintaining an overseas INS inspections staff is not an insignificant one.

Furthermore, any pre-inspections system must provide for mechanisms, including specially trained personnel, to assure that legitimate asylum seekers are afforded a meaningful opportunity to seek protection. The balancing of increased security needs and strengthened deterrence measures against terrorists with the obligation under U.S. and international law to protect those fleeing persecution must be maintained in a way that does not exclude asylum seekers from protection. Stringent pre-inspection at foreign airports much be accompanied by expanded asylum determination or "credible fear" screening, so that asylum seekers can continue to the U.S. to pursue their compelling and legitimate claims.

6. IN-FLIGHT TRANSMITTAL OF PASSENGER LISTS

Mandating at the time of take off that all airlines transmit passengers' names to the destination airport to be checked against the look out list is another important security tool. Through their reservation systems, airlines know in advance who will be flying to the U.S. Transmitting the list in advance would give U.S. authorities the opportunity to compare the passenger list to the lookout lists, thereby preventing from entering or apprehending those who should not be permitted to enter the U.S. Currently, about 75% of airlines transmit these lists.

The effectiveness of such a system also depends on the INS having adequate technology and personnel on the receiving end to make swift and efficient use of the incoming information.

If pre-inspection is conducted with meaningful safeguards to guarantee protection for asylum seekers, then the transmission of passenger lists should not compromise the safety of asylum seekers who may be en route to the U.S. Again, however, as Congress considers measures to strengthen and mandate such data collection and transmission, it must include explicit safeguards to assure meaningful access to asylum protection for those who truly need and deserve it.

7. NORTH AMERICAN PERIMETER SAFETY ZONE

To further enhance our intelligence, the U.S. needs to employ multilateral strategies with Canada and Mexico to enhance the security of all three countries to create a North American perimeter.

Such a North American perimeter will bolster security through law enforcement coordination, intelligence sharing, and better joint use of enforcement resources. Such coordination and cooperation would reduce the chance that someone wishing to do harm to the U.S. would travel to one of our neighboring countries and then cross by land into the U.S.

Beyond our immediate neighbors, the U.S. needs to more closely cooperate with our European allies in particular and share information that each of our intelligence services have collected. Consistent with the need to protect the privacy of innocent persons, we should have access to their version of the lookout lists, and reciprocate by sharing our information.

Any cooperation among governments in the region in immigration enforcement should include a plan to ensure that asylum seekers have meaningful access to protection. While Mexico has recently acceded to the refugee convention, access to asylum remains problematic, particularly for migrants intercepted at Mexico's southern border. Access to asylum procedures in Central American countries is even less assured.

On the other hand, Canada should not be pressured into diminishing protections for refugees. All countries in the region can and should strengthen security measures. However, none should be required to lower their protections for refugees to the "lowest common denominator."

As North American security cooperation also addresses the issues of smuggling and trafficking, the European experience is particularly relevant regarding protection for asylum seekers. UNHCR commissioned a report that concluded that the majority of asylum seekers arriving in the European Union have been smuggled or trafficked. The report also states that in the European Union "the effects of blanket enforcement measures, such as common visa policies, readmission treaties, carrier sanctions, and airline liaison officers (pre-inspection personnel) act to deny refugees the possibility of illegal exit from the regions of their persecution."

The report recommends that European nations review their migration and asylum policies to open other channels to people fleeing persecution in their native countries. This includes incorporating the right to seek asylum and the responsibility of non-refoulment into antitrafficking and anti-smuggling policy, recognizing that trafficking and smuggling are both "inherently abusive" and that both trafficked and smuggled persons can be refugees, improving reception conditions, and increasing family reunification.

Our government, while working with Canada, Mexico, and other partners in the region to eradicate terrorism, should also ensure that meeting the protection needs of asylum seekers is included as part of any plan.

8. ENTRY-EXIT CONTROLS

Congress needs to ensure adequate personnel and technological improvements at and between our ports of entry. The August 2001 GAO Report, "INS Southwest Border Strategy: Resource and Impact Issues Remain After Seven Years," clearly identifies that our security risks apply to both our borders.

To that end, it would be helpful to enhance our data gathering at airports by mandating an entry/exit system that would collect and correlate data about arrivals and departures. Certain airlines currently collect such information on a voluntary basis. This important security function should be government-mandated and funded. The data collected will only be useful if correlated -with better intelligence data.

An entry-exit system has been discussed for land border points of entry into the U.S. Such a system would be difficult to implement, would be exceedingly disruptive to commerce, and most importantly, would contribute little to the security of the U.S. A June 1998 report from the Senate Judiciary Committee, then chaired by Senator Orin Hatch (R–UT), noted the catastrophic delays that would accompany the implementation of a Section 110 entry-exit system at land borders. For example, the report cited testimony from an earlier hearing of a witness who estimated that "assuming the most efficient and remarkable entry and exit procedures in the world that will take only 30 seconds per vehicle, and making the equally optimistic assumption that only half the vehicles have to go through the procedures, that would amount to an extra 3,750 minutes of additional processing time each day" at the Ambassador Bridge in Detroit. The witness then pointed out that there are only 1,440 minutes to a day, which means that implementing a Section 110 entry-exit system at that land border port of entry would lead to a delay of more than 2 ½ days.

Importantly, the report also notes that it is highly questionable if implementing Section 110 would ultimately provide any assistance in prosecuting individual visa overstayers, and has nothing to do with stopping terrorists or traffickers. An automated entry-exit control system's database will in no way provide information as to which individuals might be engaging in terrorism or other unlawful activities. We must not fool ourselves into believing that implementing an entry-exit control system at land borders will increase our security: It is a false solution that will hurt our commerce and trade and not contribute to our safety.

Again, as in most forms of data collection and record keeping, the usefulness of the data is very dependent on the quality of the intelligence information with which it is correlated. Did the vast majority of these people who failed to depart on time do so for innocent reasons? Did they stay an extra week at Disney World? Did they delay departure to attend a friend's wedding, or because Grandma could not fly on account of an ear infection? Did they eventually depart, one week or two weeks or even a month late? Or are they the tiny, even miniscule minority who intend to stay to commit some heinous act of terrorism in the United States?

How do we make sense of this data that we can and will collect? Who looks at it? Who runs the cross checks, against what data bases? What do we know about someone, or what can we learn from our overseas intelligence sources that was not available when the visa was issued that will tell us whether the person is someone we should seek out and investigate? How do we find the person anyway, even if we have verified that he has not departed the United States in a timely fashion? All of these complexities must be carefully considered before Congress rushes to implement additional reporting and departure information collection or a new exit/entry control system.

AFFIRMATION OF THIS NATION'S DIVERSITY

In the current environment, it is especially important to reaffirm that this nation's strength and future reside in our unity as a nation, the diversity from which we draw our strength, and the democratic principles on which our country is based. President Bush, the Congress, and individual members of Congress, and many members of the general public all have condemned the violence directed against Arab-Americans, Muslim-Americans, and Asian-American communities by misguided people who wrongly blame these communities for the terrorists' heinous acts. We must continue to support diversity and condemn violence and hate crimes.

CONCLUSION

In conclusion, let us remember that U.S. immigration policy is based on a number of values that relate to the core social and economic principles on which our nation was founded. These values are complementary and interweave to create the rich fabric that is beneficial to all Americans. Among the most important values are:

The unification of American families;

Employment related immigration to keep America strong in a global economy;

Asylum protection for refugees fleeing persecution;

Naturalization based on allegiance to the principles contained in our Constitution and laws;

Immigration policy that is implemented through a well-regulated system based on law, with fair, uniform, and predictable requirements.

As the current situation calls out for change in the direction of more effective means of deterring terrorism, we must not lose sight of these fundamental values of this nation of immigrants. As we seek to create new means to isolate terrorists, we must take care not to isolate America in the process.

Mr. Chairman, thank you very much for this opportunity to share my thoughts and perspectives with the Committee. I and other members of AILA remain available to discuss these matters with you at any future time. We look forward to working closely with you on legislative efforts to enact these policy proposals.

Chairman KENNEDY. Very fine.

Senator BROWNBACK. Well, said.

Chairman KENNEDY. Dr. Papademetriou?

STATEMENT OF DEMETRIOS G. PAPADEMETRIOU, CO-DIRECTOR, MIGRATION POLICY INSTITUTE, WASHINGTON, D.C.

Mr. PAPADEMETRIOU. Thank you, Mr. Chairman. Good to see you again, Mr. Brownback.

I must say that I find myself in a bit of a peculiar position because your opening statement and the comments of my colleagues so far have pretty much covered most of the things that I might have said. I guess I should start with a general point which I hope that we are going to keep in the front part of our heads as we move forward with legislation and its implementation, which is that whatever it is that we opt for, it should not be policies that make us feel good; rather, they should be policies that are smart and hard-headed and can be implemented in a way that really advances our security interests. And I think an awful lot of the discussion about databases and intelligence cooperation and stovepipes and horizontal kinds of cooperation are very, very important, but I hope that we will apply this kind of a test before we would move forward with any initiatives.

As you mentioned, Mr. Chairman, most of my testimony deals with the findings and recommendations that come out of a book to be formally released at the end of this month, on the 30th. It is called "Caught in the Middle: Border Communities in an Era of Globalization." Needless to say, the research for that book was done almost in a different era, back in 1998 and 1999. It was written in the year 2000. It just happens to be released now because that it is when it came back from the publisher's.

But as we were reviewing the book, my colleague and I, Deborah Meyers, who is also my co-author, we found that there is an awful lot in that book that actually makes sense after September 11th, even more so perhaps than it made sense before the 11th.

If I were to sort of break the pattern here in my testimony and talk about an overall insight that we got from many weeks of field research, both along the U.S.–Canada border and along the U.S.–Mexico border, there is a certain resistance on the part of bureaucracies to basically ask some of the questions that I hope we need to ask them, and we will, and ask for greater accountability. In other words, we saw a certain mindlessness in a certain way of doing things simply because that was the way that they had always done things. And I think that this may indeed be the very time for us to ask ourselves how we might do things more smartly rather than how much more money can we throw at these bureaucracies.

I was very impressed with the fact that this was a major conclusion of the book, and yet that happened before the 11th of September.

I will go through about two or three out of ten major findings of the book, and I will be happy to explain those during the Q and A. But basically what we tried to find out were the answers to the following three questions: How do the NAFTA partners perceive and conduct their border inspection responsibilities? Are such inspections done in the most effective and manner—and consistent with other important public policy priorities? And what are the effects of these actions on the life of the communities that straddle NAFTA's international borders? Because, as you mentioned, Mr. Brownback, we shouldn't forget that there are other national priorities. We must protect ourselves, but we must also not sink our economy or ignore the lives of people who live in communities that straddle these borders.

Among the general findings, one is that national government policies toward border control tend to be inconsistent, even erratic, with patterns often ranging from inattention to the wrong kind of attention. And we found this to be the truth along a single border, across both borders, and sometimes simply from one port of entry to another port of entry. I hope that the events of the last month or so may focus the mind of the managers of these processes in order to at least increase consistency in the way in which we deliver those functions.

Another general finding was that the adoption of a model of tight controls and the empowerment of border officials to exclude people with little accountability have become breeding grounds for arbitrary behavior by national government personnel. They also create more opportunities for corruption and encourage the growth of market forces designed to defeat border controls.

Simply put, what this suggests is that when we come up with additional policies and when we come up with new systems that we wish to fund, we should be mindful that they are indeed the right systems and they are applied consistently and, indeed, do not defy other national priorities, which is what we found.

And a third, and I believe the last, general finding that I want to talk about is that there is a remarkable degree of community-devised cross-border cooperation on issues such as public health, access to education, environmental protection, joint regional planning, and, yes, law enforcement and security. So I hope that as we, in our capital here, are beginning to develop ways for doing things differently at the border, that somebody also is communicating with the interests within the local communities and taking their recommendations and their concerns into account, because they have many interesting ideas that may actually make us better at what it is that we are trying to do.

I wanted to quickly go through three major recommendations.

First, I think that border control should be conceptualized as a means to an end rather than as the ultimate policy goal as sometimes reflected in political rhetoric and bureaucratic initiatives. I was very pleased to hear your comments, Mr. Kennedy, because they relate precisely to this recommendation.

The second one is that all three national governments must show uncharacteristic adeptness in adapting their border management and enforcement practices to local conditions. Again, it is very, very disturbing to see using a single set of practices, a single methodology, across an entire border or, for that matter, two borders.

And the third recommendation stems from the second one, that there should not be a one-size-fits-all approach to the issues at hand, and this is an important recommendation.

Then we talk about what kinds of things we might perhaps do differently, jointly, initially with our friends in Canada and then over time, and after we test the possibility, with Mexico. And these perhaps fall a bit outside of the box. This is really thinking prospectively as to how we might do things better that serve the multiple interests that a border inspection regime must serve, not just about refugees but also about economic interests and what have you. And we have about ten or so recommendations, and we are asking for the customs agencies to try to see whether they need to perform all the functions they are performing where it is that they are performing them currently. In other words, there is now technology, a lot of it off-the-shelf technology, that can be used to seal cargos and to actually send along all the information along a variety of passageways so we don't really have to do some of those things at the border.

We should consider employing risk management strategies. The science is very well developed, and there are great opportunities for us to allow more of the resources, the limited resources that we have to be focused on bad practices and bad people rather than inconveniencing everyone, without any loss in security.

The third one involves possibly thinking about how we might do things together with our NAFTA partners, in this instance, again, Canada. Is it possible that some of the functions that the customs or the immigration agencies have to perform could be perhaps performed jointly, but performed only once, perhaps? With the right technology, the right suggestions or legislation, and the right kinds of agreements between the United States and Canada, we can be much more efficient and at least as effective in terms of our primary responsibilities and concerns. And this can, again, apply both to Immigration and to Customs.

We should also consider whether we need to staff borders with agents from different agencies like we do now between the Customs and the Immigration Service. The Canadians have as the primary inspection agency the customs agency. I am not saying whether it should be Customs or Immigration. But if you want consistent delivery in terms of the priorities that we set, why not have a single agency do the primary function, primary inspection, and then have the other agencies to do backup, secondary inspections?

Why not use the private sector—

Chairman KENNEDY. I will give you another minute or two because I want to hear from Mr. Norton, and then we will have some questions.

Mr. PAPADEMETRIOU. Okay. Why not use the private sector? We have an extensive system of customs brokers and private bondsmen. We can give them an additional responsibility and force them to be more accountable than they have been to date. And as my colleagues have mentioned, let's try to use to the fullest extent possible pre-clearance and intelligence cooperation with our colleagues in Canada and Mexico. In fact, even a common visa regime which allows each country to issue visas along the same criteria on the maximum, the largest number of countries, where that can be possible, while identifying the few areas in which we must continue to disagree, may actually provide much greater security for us than the status quo.

I will stop here, and I hope to be able to answer some of your questions.

[The prepared statement of Mr. Papademetriou follows:]

STATEMENT OF DR. DEMETRIOS G. PAPADEMETRIOU, CO-DIRECTOR AND DEBORAH WALLER MEYERS, POLICY ANALYST, MIGRATION POLICY INSTITUTE

I. INTRODUCTION

Mr. Chairman, Members of the Subcommittee. Thank you for asking me to testify today regarding border security issues and options. My name is Demetrios Papademetriou, and I am the Co-Director of the Migration Policy Institute. I am testifying on behalf of myself and my colleague Deborah Meyers.

Our testimony is based on the research and recommendations in our book, Caught in the Middle: Border Communities in an Era of Globalization. This book will be publicly released on October 30th, and is the culmination of three years of work in a comparative project studying border communities and border management issues along five different international borders U.S.-Canada, U.S.-Mexico, Germany-Poland, Russia-China, Russia-Kazakh. My remarks today, however, will focus on immigration and border issues that relate specifically to the U.S.'s neighbors and NAFTA partners, Canada and Mexico.

Clearly, our book was written well before the tragic events of September 11 and report on research conceived about three years ago, carried out primarily in 1999, and completed last year. Yet, our insights and conclusions seem to us to be remarkably relevant today. We found a troubling lack of interest in applying even the most modest "effectiveness" test to our border management methodologies. In fact, we identified no particular effort, really, not particular interest, in the independent evaluation of the dominant control methodology. More tellingly, perhaps, we identified no attempt to think systematically about whether alternative responses to the challenge might have a greater or lesser chance of success. This slavish adherence to doing "more of the same" has had several perverse effects, including papering over the human effects of the new enforcement status quo and disregarding a policy's effects on the communities in which people live and through which goods and people pass—communities that have become the terrain where the manifestations of numerous conflicting perspectives play themselves out.

It is indeed the residents, businesses, and public and private institutions of border communities who most directly absorb the costs and benefits from both freer movement and greater controls. How do these communities navigate these issues, conflicting aims and all? What is life like for those who live and work at the interface of two countries? What is the local perspective on the movement of people and goods that pass through a community; does anyone else care about it? Does the perspective vary from one community, or one border, to another, and what accounts for any variance? What input, if any, do local communities have into national policies that ultimately affect them? What creative solutions have they found to address the challenge of such policies? Our effort attempted to shed some light on all of these questions.

Two points of departure dominated our conceptualization of the research project. The first was a clear sense that, left on their own, national governments and bureaucracies would do what comes most naturally to them: national governments will reassert control (particularly when feeling a degree of threat) and the relevant agencies will seek to convert such fears into additional resources, growing in size and influence. The effectiveness of the effort, however, seems to have only an uncertain association with the resources committed to border controls. Somewhat paradoxically, saturation policing and other forms of vigorous control seem to produce numerous perverse by-products, including a boom in official corruption and the growth in powerful black markets in virtually all aspects relating to the defeat of the control effort-from false documents to sophisticated smuggling networks. (Notwithstanding that tendency, our research found local cross-border initiatives continue to occur, even flourish, under all of these scenarios.)

The second was an idea that many border communities had become concerned with the fact that decisions that affect them directly on issues of borders and their management were being made without their participation. In an era of pronounced devolution, much of it admittedly more rhetorical than real, that decision locus exclusively in the national capitals, with little pretense of consultation with local communities-struck us as worthy of further investigation. We suspected that the continuing function of borders as the physical location where real and symbolic expressions of state sovereignty meet probably explained why domestic decisions about them are seemingly made "unilaterally" by central governments.

Our overall conclusion? Unless the politics make it absolutely impossible, governments are better off working cooperatively and with the market to expand the legal means for the entry of their nationals in other states' territories. Acknowledging the economic and social facts on the ground and regulating a practice thoughtfully, stand a much better chance of achieving important public-policy goals than denying the legitimacy of some of the reasons for the practice's existence and trying to stamp it out through force.

II. RESEARCH AIMS AND FINDINGS

A state performs an array of inspection functions at the border, many of which are clearly essential to good government and all which serve some public interest. This fact, however, does not obviate the need to ask whether the functions are all essential, whether they can be done only at the border, whether the manner in which they are done is the most appropriate one, and how the lives of border communities are affected by how functions are delivered. Most importantly, perhaps, and like most governmental functions that are both very costly and intrusive, the delivery of the functions itself demands that the relevant agencies meet stringent effectiveness and accountability standards. The research considered three broad policy questions:

1. How do the NAFTA partners perceive and conduct their border "inspection" responsibilities?
2. Are such inspections done in the most effective and efficient manner (and consistent with other important public policy priorities)?
3. What are the effects of these actions on the life of communities that straddle NAFTA's international borders?

Maintaining a focus on border community life as a consistent priority across all research sites, we focused on three outcomes.

1. Cataloguing and understanding existing local initiatives toward greater cooperation between border communities located on different sides of an international border;
2. uunderstanding better the similarities and differences in that regard among such communities; and
3. Extracting and contextualizing "best practices" in local self-management with regard to cross-border matters.

Field research results were then used to assess and develop a perspective on the state of integration within North America, and particularly within the North American Free Trade Agreement space, and to articulate a vision for such integration in fifteen or twenty years.

The project's principal research hypothesis was that at the local level, communities on both sides of a common border were thinking (and when allowed, acting) creatively and often collaboratively in response to common problems and in pursuit of common interests. Although the degree of cooperation and the motives for cooperation vary significantly across borders and border regions, in almost all instances examples of cooperation were found to exist-thus validating the hypothesis.

The following are among the most robust general findings of the research.

1. The interests of border regions typically receive inadequate and at times unwelcome attention from national governments. This is typically due to the fact that central governments think of their responsibilities toward borders within the framework of "reasons of state." The post-September 1 I environment makes this point more starkly than we could have hypothesized. Such thinking, especially when "security" concerns enter the mix, reinforces the tendency of bureaucracies to make decisions unilaterally and leads to the devaluation of local dynamics and preferences. For instance, along the U.S.Mexico border, anxiety about drugs and unauthorized immigration has led to fortifications and an active policing framework that gives short shrift to the border's other principal function: facilitation of legal traffic and trade.

2. National government policies toward border control tend to be inconsistent, even erratic, with patterns often ranging,from inattention to the "wrong kind" of attention. Both extremes kindle discontent and, except in emergencies, both can generate calls for more autonomy on transborder issues of greatest concern to a locality or region. Communities along many of the borders we studied desire greater autonomy. In many instances, however, communities make fundamentally contradictory demands. For instance, along the U.S. southwest border, many U.S. communities, while calling for greater order and security, simultaneously call for easier commercial access to consumers and to workers from across the border.

3. Most central governments use symbols and language that reinforce the imagery of borders as "zones of exclusion. " One is often struck by the lengths to which some governments go to establish and demarcate their state's distinctness and identity-from the display of massive flags to the creation of a no-man's-land and the building of actual fortifications. Such views, however, often contrast sharply with those of the locals, who are much more likely to consider the border a place of commercial, social, and cultural interface, part of an often single community-some of which just happens to be in a foreign political jurisdiction. Many communities along both U.S. borders feel (and act) this way.

4. The adoption of a model of tight controls and the empowerment of border officials to exclude people with little accountability have become breeding grounds for arbitrary behavior by national government personnel; they also create more opportunities for corruption and encourage the growth of market forces designed to defeat border controls. Nowhere is this phenomenon more evident than along the U.S. southwest border, although behavior at other borders follows the same general rule. As an example of arbitrariness, U.S. immigration officials at different crossings seem to interpret their authority to exclude inadmissible entrants quite differently, resulting in dramatically different outcomes. With regard to official corruption,

international smuggling networks are now widely thought to be able to corrupt government officials virtually anywhere.

5. Border communities typically approach both the challenges and the opportunities of deeper cross-border relations in a remarkably pragmatic fashion. Communities along the U.S.-Canada border typify this behavior, although below the radar screen of newspaper headlines and the rhetoric of politicians this is now a nearly universal phenomenon along uncontested borders. In fact, as cross-border contacts increase, local officials from both sides, in partnership with business interests, religious organizations, and community-based and other nongovernmental actors, seek to play increasingly significant roles in the ongoing discussions about and the making and implementation of policies that affect their lives. Clearly, not all communities are equally active in this regard and few are successful in influencing their fate in measurable ways. However, the existence of institutional frameworks that encourage and formalize input, can make a significant difference in outcomes. Two other factors also facilitate better cross-border understanding: the growth in cross-border civil society contacts, and official efforts to consider local perspectives along borders.

6. Business and commercial interests are the drivers of better cross-border relations across all research sites. In fact, some observers argue that many border communities share a single business culture in what often amounts to symbiotic, even single, markets. This holds true regardless of the degree to which business contacts are formal or informal. Not everyone shares the enthusiasm of commercial interests for more 5 cross-border openness, however, and, as a result, the vision of cross-border relations promoted by business interests can complicate matters when it is in conflict either with that of other local interests or with national priorities and regulations. Such conflicts are further exacerbated when national regulations, and/or the way in which they are implemented by representatives of national bureaucracies at the border, are internally contradictory or are thought to be at significant variance with the broader local economic life. At times, local communities seek to take initiatives to redress the perceived imbalance.

7. There is a remarkable degree of community-devised cross-border cooperation on issues such as public health, access to education, environmental protection, joint regional planning, and law enforcement. In most instances, such cooperation seems to be unaffected by the ups and downs of the national conversation on borders and, more precisely, the conversation within the national capital. Local concerns about the tone and flavor of these conversations have been heightened by a growing appreciation that discussions about borders inside national capitals seem always either to over- or under react to the real issues. Community views, on the other hand, are typically closer to the facts on the ground than is political rhetoric, and are better attuned to local needs and nuances. These range from a finer sense of increasingly common destinies and, perhaps to a lesser degree, human and ethnic solidarity.

8. Investments in the economic and social development of border regions and cities are at best an intermittent affair and tend to be inadequate even in the best of circumstances. Models of how to invest in a border region include the distribution of significant funds through supranational institutions (the EU "Euro-regions" model) and the potentially very significant U.S. investments in transportation corridors which allow investments in Canada and Mexico. A third potential model is the embryonic U.S. development efforts at its southwest border by the Interagency Task Force for the Economic Development of the Southwest Border, impaneled by the Clinton Administration. A final model comes from the Pacific Northwest, where remarkably well-organized cross-border public/private efforts have been able to make considerable progress in securing funding from state, local, and U.S. federal sources to pursue the objective of adapting national policies to the region's unique requirements and opportunities.

9. There is an increasing array of experiments with a variety of "extraterritorial" arrangements designed to facilitate commercial and socio-cultural interests. For instance, the United States has experimented with permitting Mexican border inspection functions to be performed deep within U.S. territory during the Christmas season (in order to reduce delays at the border as large numbers of Mexicans return home for the holidays). The United States and Mexico have reciprocally expanded the zone for the less restricted movement of Mexicans in Arizona to 65 miles (and for Americans into Sonora for 100 kilometers), mostly as a means of encouraging access by Mexican nationals to U.S. commercial establishments. Finally, in most major Canadian airports, the United States has a deeply institutionalized pre-clearance system for customs, immigration, and associated agencies for travelers to the United States, and together with Canada it is taking the first tentative steps toward sharing inspection facilities and related items.

10. Next to being given short shrift by national authorities and the lack of resources, lack of "capacity" may be the border communities' greatest problem. It may be difficult to overemphasize this point. The capacity gap spans the gamut of activities along borders. It is clearly more pronounced in poorer countries, in remote border communities, and in the communities most recently delegated political power. It also exists, however, in communities lacking sufficient physical capacity to handle the ever expanding traffic. The need for capacity building goes beyond governance and beyond the public sector, including the fields of education and health services and the development of a culture of civil society that can hold the government accountable for its decisions and can play a part in the development of a broader base of social activism.

III. RECOMMENDATIONS

The rich and intricate tapestry of complex interdependence stitched together by the case studies in this volume makes clear that generalizations and, ultimately, policy recommendations need to exercise extreme care not to oversimplify. The case studies also make clear, however, that there is a great deal more going with cross-border communities than many analysts have suspected and, more to the point, than either national leaders or the national press have bothered to recognize.

What, then, might one recommend that is consistent with and moves toward the more open and cooperative future the research results discussed in this volume imply? We are making three overall recommendations.

1. Border controls should be conceptualized as a means to an end, rather than as the ultimate policy goal portrayed in political rhetoric and reflected in bureaucratic initiatives. Put differently, the explicit end-goal of regulatory and enforcement efforts at the border should be to manage the border effectively enough to prepare the ground for the serious conversation about how best jointly to accomplish each neighbor's principal public policy priorities while allowing more organic forms of integration to proceed at a reasonable pace. One implication of this recommendation is that the current set of discussions and initiatives regarding the NAFTA partners' internal borders should continue to proceed roughly along the paths they have been following in the last year or so; this must be accompanied, however, by an explicit reconceptualization and articulation of the desirable endpoint. Focusing squarely on the greater use of technology and on management innovations that improve both facilitation and regulation and control must be part and parcel of this process-but, again, they must not be the end points of the NAFTA relationships.

For the U.S.-Canada border, continuing along the path of the last year or so but with a re-conceptualization of the end point means ever-closer and more organic cooperation, a more explicit focus on understanding and addressing differences, and far greater experimentation. For the U.S.-Mexico border, this means that Mexico's deeper engagement of the United States over the last year or so must not just continue in earnest but in fact must accelerate further, and it must shift gears. This bilateral relationship is too important for either country to become distracted by the differences between them.

Although that engagement's centerpiece is the migration relationship, the border cannot be left too far behind-if for no other reason than that it is deeply intertwined with the migration issue.

2. All three national governments must show uncharacteristic adeptness in

adapting their border management and enforcement practices to local conditions. While in the U.S. context this recommendation may raise important field-management concerns about the U.S. Immigration and Naturalization Service (which has proven unable to rein in its field managers and deliver many of its functions with consistency), the principle nonetheless remains a powerful one. Whenever possible, field managers should be encouraged to work in tandem with local communities to deliver the various components of the immigration function in a manner that is sensitive to and builds upon the particular circumstances of an area.

Currently, hardly any border communities have either a strategy or a mechanism for building their capacity to aggregate and articulate their interests. (The U.S.-Canada border may be the only near-exception.) Developing such strategies and investing in mechanisms-such as a regular annual or biennial meeting of public and private-sector interests along and across a single border-could address this weakness. Such a regular forum would institutionalize the exchange of views, facilitate the process of learning about each other's interests, priorities, successes, and failures, and offer an opportunity to build relationships and impanel issue-focused groups, as appropriate, to promote common interests.

Central governments also should initiate regular, systematic opportunities for local interests to be brought into the decision-making process about issues that affect them. Such an initiative would address a second systemic weakness of the status quo the lack of a formal mechanism for communities to convey their interests to the appropriate central government policy-making bodies in a manner that is timely and thus enhances the prospects of a fair hearing.

3. There should not be a one-size-fits-all approach to the issues at hand not even along a single border. History, topography, economy, and the level of local engagement with the issue (both that of the public sector and that of the for-profit and not-for-profit private sectors), lead to enormous variability in the delivery of border inspection functions, as do differences in outlooks and management and the personal skills of the local managers of national bureaucracies. These differences demand, and sometimes in fact result in, sensitive and thoughtful approaches that respect and take advantage of differences. These approaches, however, still need to be informed by a single policy frame of reference and must reflect the levels of shared goals and objectives between the two countries-that is, building upon, rather than undermining, the increasingly seamless cooperation between the two countries in a vast array of policy areas.

The importance of policy clarity and, more importantly, of policies that have a real purpose-an end-goal or a vision-cannot be overemphasized, nor can its absence, from virtually every border this project has studied, be more pronounced. It is, in our view, the most fundamental explanation for the relative state of confusion about the management of borders, and for the inconsistency with which it is proceeding. As a result of this failure of imagination, states do not seem able to learn from and successfully incorporate innovations in managing borders, or in testing different management models and alternative methodologies.

IV. THE VOLUME'S NORTH AMERICAN VISION

We call on the three NAFTA partners to commence initially domestic processes to develop a strategic plan for changing the terms of the debate about the border relationship with their immediate neighbors. Whatever is agreed to must proceed from the assumption that if negotiations are to succeed, they must recommend activities that are gradual and evolutionary, and in each instance take into account the interests of the affected communities. This implies much deeper levels of national government/state (provincial) and local government cooperation. It also implies far greater and more systematic consultations with local stakeholders than any of the three national governments is either familiar with or perhaps comfortable in undertaking.

Our vision imagines the NAFTA's internal borders gradually (and in temporal and substantive terms, unevenly) becoming irrelevant to the point where their abolition could proceed without any measurable losses in any of the important security, revenue collection, and even "identity" priorities of each partner, at least relative to the results of the present course of action. The vision also imagines small actual additional losses in "sovereignty" for any of the partners. Any such "losses," in fact, would in our view be offset by substantial democratic surpluses for all three NAFTA partners.

Such a vision could be best approached from two distinct, yet ultimately converging, tracks. Both require greater vertical and horizontal consciousness-raising and greater and more systematic input by local communities and their institutions-public and private. The first track focuses on continuing the multiplicity of contacts, the deepening of bilateral engagement, and the focus on pragmatic problem-solving that has been the operational model for the past few years-if intermittently so. The second track should focus on the kind of North America the citizens of the three countries have a legitimate right to expect in the not-too-distant future-and on how best to achieve it.

Some of this latter track's required elements will of necessity be "defensive" in nature; that is, they must "protect" citizens from unwanted activities, practices, and products. Other elements will be forward-looking and will be advancing broader citizen interests in terms of prosperity, adherence to rules, protection of rights, and fundamental conformity with the principles of humanitarianism. In its totality, the proposed vision should hold the promise for doing better by most people in each of the NAFTA partners along most of these goals.

Such a vision should include the following among its main elements:

1. Greater security from illegal activities and unwanted products from outside the NAFTA space-including terrorism, illegal immigration, drugs, and more;
2. Protection from illegal activities and undesirable products that may be found inside the NAFTA region that will be no less reliable than what each NAFTA partner enjoys now;

3. The nearly seamless movement of legitimate goods and people seeking to cross internal NAFTA borders; and
4. Protection from the political ups and downs (the political "mood swings," as it were) of one NAFTA partner or another and, perhaps more importantly, from bureaucratic "ad-hocism," affecting the vital interests of the other partners.

Is our vision realistic-particularly in the post-September 11 environment? We think so. Will critics think that it is realistic? Probably not. In many ways, there are few things easier than shooting down a vision. The three NAFTA capitals are full of people who know how to say "no" a million ways. (Bureaucracies of all types are particularly adept at saying "no" to changes in their mission or culture. Ultimately, since it is bureaucracies that will implement any vision, working with them will bear more fruit than working against them.) Getting to "yes," however, requires great political courage and uncommon qualities of leadership. Nor can a vision of a different future immediately provide fully satisfactory answers to all the questions-legitimate or not-that one may pose. Realizing the vision proposed here will be rocky and the outcome frequently will seem uncertain. Furthermore, as with the early stages of any ambitious new initiative, there will be winners and losers-and each NAFTA partner will have to give priority to developing and implementing, policies that address the concerns of those who will likely lose at the beginning.

V. SOME INITIATIVES THAT CANADA AND THE U.S. CAN BEGIN TO IMPLEMENT AS SOON AS POSSIBLE

Integration is a gradual process involving a myriad of incremental steps and the building of trust. To begin, we suggest that each border inspection agency be required to analyze each one of the functions it performs at the border along four lines: First, must each of its functions be done only at the border? Second, what are the costs and benefits of doing that function at the border versus doing it elsewhere? Third, can any of its functions be performed by an inspector from a sister agency? Fourth, can any of the functions in question be performed (after proper negotiations, training, etc.) by an inspector from the other country?

We list below some concrete steps in the process of rethinking border management. We expect these initiatives to be tested first with Canada but expect that, over time, those that pass the tests, would be gradually "exported" to the U.S.-Mexico border.

• Customs could perform many of its inspections and collect all applicable duties at the point where the cargo is loaded in North America, employing available technology to "seal" the containers) and transferring all the relevant information about the cargo electronically to any other inspection point.

• Customs could employ "risk-management" methodologies for performing inspection functions and re-deploy some of the newly "released" personnel to joint investigative task forces with sister agencies from either side of the border in order to uncover violations of various types.

• One NAFTA partner could handle inspections and the collection of tariffs on behalf of the others or could do so jointly-but always once-at the initial point in which a cargo from a non-NAFTA country enters NAFTA space. Similarly, progress should be made on the "unified port management" concept for its potential to use resources most efficiently while improving both service and the quality of inspections.

• Border customs inspections could be done only once-by either national customs service-so as to accommodate variances in staffing, physical infrastructure, and topographical idiosyncrasies.

• The United States could copy the Canadian model of having only one agency staff the primary inspection lanes, rather than having both Customs and the Immigration and Naturalization Service. All necessary inspection agencies would still retain a presence at the border to perform secondary inspections.

• Existing systems of customs brokers and private bondsmen could be utilized to a far greater extent and given both greater power and greater responsibility-and, by extension, made more accountable (and penalized more severely) for failures - of either omission or commission.

• The private sector could be relied upon even more consequentially in areas ranging from technology to the building of better infrastructure wherever it might be needed, through liberalized public-private partnerships and pay-as-you-go projects.

• The INS could handle all third-country (non-NAFTA) immigration controls at an individual's first point of entry into NAFTA space. Pre-clearance technology and intelligence cooperation are in many instances already significant enough to expect that this method can be accelerated without any loss of control relative to 11 the status quo. In fact, airport inspections are more accurate and can be more efficient than virtually any system of inspections at land borders, where visa and identity checks, even after September 11.

- Canada and the United States could agree to a common visa regime for the widest band of countries each country could accommodate and exercise much greater care in the issuance of visas for the citizens of countries for which visa-free entry could not be agreed to by the other country.
- Canada and the United States initially, the U.S. and Mexico at a later point, and, eventually, all three NAFTA partners and contiguous neighbors, could gradually liberalize the movement of each other's nationals, thus freeing their inspection resources to focus more on non-NAFTA nationals. (It is worth noting that despite having reached absolute freedom of movement, intra-EU migration by EU citizens is minuscule, at between seven and eight million persons, or about two percent of the EU's population.) Potential exploitation of a country's social support systems by nationals of another NAFTA country can be addressed up front in a variety of ways, including requiring departure within a specific time period if a job or other means of support hasn't been found or by continuing the social protection mechanisms of the country of origin for the initial few months after entry.

These recommendations are not made in a vacuum. Some tentative steps toward the directions recommended here are already being taken, the technology is readily available, and the large business sector that accounts for most of the transborder initiatives and energy is thought to be fully primed for cooperating in return for more timely and predictable results. A vision, and political will, seem to be the major missing ingredients.

We must also note that our vision has no room for supranational bureaucracies a la Brussels. We believe instead in an integration process that is organic and is thus built from the bottom up-and from the periphery to the center, that is, from border regions to capital cities, differing dramatically from the top-down approach the EU practices even today. Europe's experience nonetheless reminds us that progress on even the most intractable issues comes down to creativity, leadership, local input, an overarching vision, - liberal amounts of common sense, and a willingness to experiment and learn from others.

VI. CONCLUDING THOUGHTS

Few issues in the international system are as complex as those surrounding borders. As this volume demonstrates, the roots of that complexity include but go beyond the reality that borders are the most direct physical manifestation of "statehood" and sovereignty. They also are inextricably linked with competing policy priorities that simultaneously expect border inspection systems to allow the swift and efficient passage of legitimate people and products while unerringly stopping illegitimate traffic and undesirable products. At their very root, however, borders and their "management" or "protection," however much these last functions may have changed in recent years, are first and foremost political concepts, and can only be addressed politically.

What relationships, then, might one anticipate within the NAFTA-space in the years ahead? Canada's understandable preoccupation with its U.S. relationship will continue to motivate that country to ensure by any means necessary that the economic relationship continues to grow in ways that guarantee the prosperity of its people. It is in fact our contention that, substantively at least, the U.S.-Canada border is likely to disappear before any politician finds the political courage to negotiate its removal. Symbolic issues, of course, will need to be addressed, as will the significant strengthening of police functions both along the outside perimeter of North America and-an important policy development-in the interior of each country, an intensification that is already occurring.

Mexico, buoyed by and ready to draw on the democratic dividend created by Mr. Fox's defeat of the candidate of the Institutional Revolutionary Party (PRI) in the 2000 presidential elections, has found the confidence to enter into bilateral negotiations with the United States about a tough binational "bargain" on migration and border issues. That bargain, whenever the post-September 11 climate allows it to move forward, would offer Mexicans much greater access to the part of the U.S. economy and labor markets in which it is already a major player in return for far greater and much more active cooperation in addressing the primarily "law-and-order" issues of concern to the United States. Mexico's ability to deliver on the responsibilities it would undertake under such a bargain would in turn determine the pace at which it may begin to catch up with the U.S. treatment of the U.S.-Canada border.

Finally, U.S. interest in the North American "project" envisioned here ("acceptance" may be a more appropriate term than "interest ") is likely to be tepid until it is convinced that it can accomplish its own policy priorities less expensively, more efficiently, and much more effectively than under the status quo. In that regard, it is the limits of thicker and infinitely more expensive unilateral controls that may persuade the United States to consider truly alternative ways of dealing with these issues.

Mr. Chairman, Members of the Subcommittee: Ensuring our safety requires a comprehensive, system-wide response that goes well beyond the jurisdiction of this Subcommittee and includes not only the INS but each and every public agency with which foreign entrants interact. Our nation's security from foreign nationals who may wish us ill in the months and years ahead rests on the simultaneous and sustained pursuit of several initiatives.

This is an extraordinary task under any circumstances; it becomes even more so, however, given our record as a people of a generally low attention span on matters large and small. This tendency makes it all the more important that we resist the twin impulsions of (1) throwing money at the problem (this problem is too large and it can "break the bank" rather quickly) and (2) rushing to create new and cumbersome data 13 systems that may offer only marginal benefits to the common objective of making our country more secure while having enormous long term costs on who we are as a nation.

Based on our research, we believe that, over time, we can achieve many more of our goals working together with the intelligence gathering and law-enforcement agencies of our allies in this "war on terrorism," and particularly with those of our North American partners-Canada and Mexico than we can do unilaterally. Seamless cooperation in protecting our common North American space, what some people now call "perimeter defense," is a goal worth pursuing at a pace and with as much vigor as prudence and the capabilities of each of our partners allow.

Ultimately, Mr. Chairman, we can protect ourselves better through "external" controls, that is, actions that we might take before an undesirable alien gains entry into our country than "internal" controls, that is, measures taken once one has been admitted. Put differently, keeping undesirable individuals out of the US through "front gate controls" (that is, the visa issuance and border inspection regimes), is both easier and more effective than attempting to catch up with such persons after they enter the US. Focusing most of our additional resources on prevention measures demands that we treat our contiguous neighbors as the assets that they are (and can be) than as the liabilities that some seek to make them.

Thank you, Mr. Chairman, for the opportunity to appear before you and the Subcommittee.

Chairman KENNEDY. Thank you very much.

Mr. Norton?

STATEMENT OF RICHARD E. NORTON, EXECUTIVE DIRECTOR, INTERNATIONAL BIOMETRIC INDUSTRY ASSOCIATION, FAIRFAX, VIRGINIA

Mr. NORTON. Mr. Chairman, Senator Brownback, thanks for the opportunity to appear here today before this panel.

We are pleased to note the consensus we have seen today on the need for greater use of biometrics and understand the crucial role they can play. In the past, we think the biometrics have been largely misconstrued as perhaps invasive technologies that would be compromising privacy when, in fact, the opposite is the case, and we are seeing a broad recognition of that—really the only way to offer a technological silver bullet here, to coin a phrase used by Mr. Ziglar, that can offer security, that can offer convenience, and also protect privacy at the same time.

The reason is that biometrics are stored as encrypted digital information. They are not stored as an image, with rare exception, and they can't be reverse-engineered to reveal anything about the holder. They don't say anything about the sex, the age, the race of the person's identity, and they can truly place a lock and key on this information and protect it from prying eyes.

Our message is simple: The U.S. has the tools to immediately implement several important biometric-based programs and make a difference right away. By consolidating information, placing the proper equipment in the field, and enabling real-time checks of the data, valid document holders can be identified at any stage of the process, from application at a consular post to departure from the United States.

Our recommendations are to do the following now:

First, deploy readers at the border that can verify the identity of any holder of an alien resident card or border crossing card. By the end of next year, there will be nearly 20 million of these documents in circulation, and all have biometric information securely embedded in them. This information can be relied on to determine if a holder is properly linked to the document at the time they apply for admission to the United States.

Second, we strongly urge the consolidation of all photo images from all U.S. travel documents into the Interagency Border Inspection System. Right now we have access to visa information that is slowly coming on at several ports of entry, and we are pleased to hear that this information may be available more broadly in the future. However, U.S. passport information is not in this database, nor is information reliably accessed on ARC holders, that is, alien resident card holders, and border crosser card holders. Doing so would give the U.S. authorities the immediate ability to verify the identity of any document holder.

And, third, we would like to recommend something that perhaps wouldn't be seen as a replacement for the pre-inspection program, but could certainly be made available universally, which pre-inspection never will be, and that is to add the images of suspected terrorists to this database that we are talking about to the Interagency Border Inspection System and make this a real-time system, driven by facial recognition technology that can be used to verify the validity of a document and the identity of the holder before the travelers board the flight to the United States. Making the Advance Passenger Information program universal is a good step, but it does nothing to stop a terrorist at the airline gate.

Real-time access using facial recognition technology can accomplish this goal while offering convenience, privacy, and security to the traveler and without resorting to something so dramatic as a national I.D. card.

There are additional steps underway. The FBI is looking at how it can improve its automated fingerprint identification system to provide the sorts of checks that are envisioned in S. 1452, introduced by the chairman last month. The U.S. Government and other governments, along with airlines, airports, and technology providers, are cooperating with the Simplifying Passenger Travel program to try to rope in as many bona fide travelers into a system of biometric identification as possible and do this on an international basis.

Third, the International Civil Aviation Organization is also trying to improve the documentation, being able to use biometrics in a passport to validate who a traveler is, again, deterring fraud, enabling us to identify people who shouldn't be in the system, and facilitating the people who should be allowed to pass freely.

Finally, we would like to add we have heard much here today about the concern about privacy. As we explained, biometric technologies do offer the ability to retain privacy without eroding security. Ultimately, the citizens' trust is going to have to be acquired by assurances that these systems are properly regulated and properly maintained. The biometric industry has been very aggressive about this and has advocated controls for several years that would enable this sort of system to be implemented with full confidence of the citizens of the United States.

Our recommendations are completely detailed in our written testimony, Senator, and we would be happy to answer any questions about them. Thank you.

[The prepared statement of Mr. Norton follows:]

STATEMENT OF RICHARD E. NORTON, EXECUTIVE DIRECTOR, INTERNATIONAL BIOMETRIC INDUSTRY ASSOCIATION

Mr. Chairman and members of the Subcommittee, thank you for inviting the biometric industry to offer its views at this important proceeding. My name is Richard E. Norton, and I am the Executive Director of the International Biometric Industry Association (IBIA). IBIA is based in Washington, D.C. and represents the collective interests of manufacturers and developers of biometric technology.

BIOMETRIC TECHNOLOGY

Biometrics are defined as the automatic identification or identity verification of an individual based on physiological or behavioral characteristics. The authentication of identity is accomplished by using computer technology in a noninvasive way to match patterns of live individuals in real time against enrolled records. Examples of the patterns used for biometric identification include those made from a finger image, the geometry of the hand, an iris, voice, signature, or face. It is important to note that most biometric applications do not store the actual image of the feature being measured. Instead, biometrics secure systems and protect an individual's identity by converting the measurement into an encrypted file. This biometric record cannot be reverse engineered to determine a person's age, sex, race or other sensitive information. Likewise, it cannot be used to steal someone's identity.

With these characteristics, biometrics are the only technologies that can offer both increased security and greater convenience. The U.S. Government has been an early adopter of biometrics, first using the devices to control access to highly sensitive facilities such as nuclear power plants and weapons facilities. Now biometrics are routinely employed to protect networks against intrusion by hackers, to secure records from identity theft, to ensure benefits are disbursed to the lawful recipient, and to protect borders.

BIOMETRICS AND BORDER CLEARANCE

The U.S. has nearly a decade of experience with this latter application. The Immigration & Naturalization Service has experimented with biometric technologies at land and air ports of entry, and has deployed its INSPASS automated kiosks at a number of major airports in the U.S. and at immigration pre-clearance sites in Canada. While the INSPASS system has not been implemented on a broad enough scale to reduce the burden on the INS inspection mission, it is widely regarded as a successful experiment that has worked as planned—in complete security—for over eight years. Other countries have had similar results: Canada, the Netherlands, Singapore, and Israel have implemented biometrics in this demanding national security role and found them to be robust and effective.

The question is how we take these low volume trials and efficiently convert the lessons learned into a comprehensive system of controls that tighten our border without causing service levels to deteriorate to unacceptable levels. Fortunately, the tools are in place to accomplish this goal: not only are the technologies reliable and standards in place, but in several significant areas the U.S. has taken preliminary steps that will enable us to make a measurable difference at a reasonable cost. Furthermore, we are convinced there are ways to accomplish our objectives at the border without having to resort to a national identity card.

ELEMENTS OF A SOLUTION

In many respects the U.S. has the key elements of biometric-based systems in place, ready to be converted into information that can be tapped to identify travelers at ports of entry, applicants at visa issuance posts overseas, and potential threats to national security as they attempt to enter or move about the country.

First, INS has issued over five million of its highly secure Alien Resident Cards (ARC) to permanent residents of the U.S. The Department of State has used the same technology on nearly five million Border Grosser Cards (BCC) that have been issued to Mexican citizens since 1999. By the end of 2002, over 20 million such cards will be in circulation; by 2007, all ARCS will have been converted to the new format. Both cards contain an image of the bearer's fingerprint that is encoded in the optical zone of the card—a feature analogous to the appearance and storage capacity of a CD–ROM, but with strong built-in encryption that has effectively prevented forgery.

Second, all U.S. visas are produced from a digital file that includes an image of the bearer. This image is now retained in State Department files and, as with the image of the ARC or BCC holder, can be used to help verify the identity of the person presenting the visa through face recognition technology.

Third, border agencies have established a nearly universal system for checking on the identity of passengers as they travel to the U.S. The Advance Passenger Information System (APIS) calls for airlines to forward biographical information to the Interagency Border Inspection System, where lookouts are run and ports notified if U.S. authorities want to closely examine a particular passenger. IBIS, if it is converted to a real time, two-way communication system and expanded to include automated links to ARC, BCC and passport data, can be used to validate the identity of travelers before they board their flight to the U.S. (see "Recommendations" below).

Fourth, the biometric industry has worked diligently to establish the standards needed for true interoperability. In cooperation with the National Institute of Standards & Technology, IBIA has created a registry that enables any biometric device to be recognized on a network. The industry and government also have worked together to publish rules on how biometrics are to be integrated into computer operating systems. . This is an exceptionally important advancement for several reasons:

- It allows multiple biometrics to be accommodated;
- It allows the quick adoption of new biometric technologies as they are developed in the future;
- It permits the rapid exchange of information for record checks; and
- It enables the use of biometric information that has been acquired by other sources, such as employers, airlines, and government agencies.

RECOMMENDATIONS

With these pieces in place, there are a number of steps that can be taken immediately to improve our capacity to properly identify people who are arriving at U.S. borders:

DEPLOY OPTICAL CARD AND FINGER IMAGE READERS.

ARCS and BCCs contain a finger image of the bearer. This image can be extracted from the card by an optical card reader, and compared to the "live" image of the person applying for admission to the U.S. by using a low-cost finger image reader. The card is virtually immune to compromise, and the process can be conducted without having to establish a network connection to a central database.

STANDARDIZE THE RETENTION OF, AND CENTRALIZE, DIGITAL IMAGES FOR ALL U.S. DOCUMENTS.

U.S. visa, ARC and BCC records contain digital images of the bearer that, if centralized, can be used to verify the identity of the traveler. The same process could be used to link U.S. passports to their holders if the Department of State updates its system to include the digital image of bearers of that document. If this information is made available through IBIS, U.S. border authorities can have real-time access to images of all applicants for admission, with the exception of travelers entering under the Visa Waiver Program.

APPLY THE USE OF FACE RECOGNITION TECHNOLOGY TO AUTOMATE THE IDENTIFICATION OF U.S. DOCUMENT HOLDERS.

As an extension of the centralization process described above, any image that is stored in the system can be used to generate a face recognition template. This template can be compared to the template that is produced by scanning the image on a travel document, or by using an image from a video camera.

EXTEND THE DOCUMENT VERIFICATION PROCESS TO THE AIRLINE CHECK-IN COUNTER.

Any system of border control and terrorist interdiction requires airlines to be an intrinsic and effective-part of the process. Currently, airlines have little to go on to determine if a traveler may be improperly documented, or if a passenger poses a danger to the aircraft. Being able to verify the identity of a U.S. document holder—or compare a suspect against a terrorist database—will enable resources to be focused on identifying those who cannot be quickly verified against accurate records. Such improvements to our current screening processes can be made by centralizing data and images in IBIS, upgrading that system to enable near-real-time interactive messaging between government and airlines, and by expanding the use of advanced, "full field of view" document readers that can automatically scan all of the information on the travel document data page.

OTHER INITIATIVES

Other programs are certain to follow these first steps in building an effective system for screening visa applicants and streamlining the admission of bona fide visitors, U.S. citizens and returning residents. Improvements to the Federal Bureau of Investigation Automated Fingerprint Identification System can expedite the kind of record checks envisioned in Senate Bill 1452, which was introduced by the Chairman of this Subcommittee on September 21, 2001; cooperative efforts such as the multi-stakeholder Simplifying Passenger Travel initiative, sponsored by the International Air Transport Association, will help the U.S. to identify a broader range of bona fide travelers who have been vetted through biometric control systems implemented in other countries; and further standardization on the use and storage of biometrics on passports under the auspices of the International Civil Aviation Organization (ICAO) will make counterfeiting, identity theft, and imposter fraud more difficult for those with ill intent.

In closing, the industry would like to mention its efforts to pursue these innovations without eroding the privacy and civil liberties of American citizens, and without disrupting international commerce. Biometric data is inherently secure and serves as a digital lock and key on personal information; but ultimately the success of these systems will depend on a traveler's trust that they will be administered responsibly. The industry's policies and guidelines on how to implement biometrics without diminishing public confidence is described in detail at our website, www.ibia.org.

Thank you again, Mr. Chairman, for this opportunity to participate in this distinguished panel. I would be pleased to answer any questions you have about these recommendations, or about biometric applications in general.

Chairman KENNEDY. Just before coming to other questions, on this issue of privacy could you just elaborate on that? What are you talking about in terms of people having a sense that in the biometric system their privacy issues are going to be preserved or protected?

Mr. NORTON. Well, as we explained, biometrics do protect privacy by their nature because they are an encrypted file and they can serve as a lock and key on personal information.

That being said, people still are concerned about biometric information being stored. To say don't worry, trust technology that it is taking care of you is an irresponsible statement to make.

So an industry, what we say is that even if these technologies have these inherent securities, then you should have a system by which they are administered. You should have careful controls over the access to the database. You should let people know what the data is being used for. They should know how it is being shared.

They should have control over its sharing if it is not for the explicit purpose of these controls. And there should be careful regulation of how they are administered, penalties imposed if people abuse this information.

Chairman KENNEDY. Okay. Could you provide some examples of the technology that is currently available and could be implemented by the INS? What are the costs involved in implementing this system? You discussed applying facial recognition technology to automate the identification of documents. What is the cost and what is the time and what are the principal sort of elements if the country was to make a judgment to go in this direction?

Mr. NORTON. There are many biometric technologies that can be used, and many are very effective at solving this problem. There is iris recognition, voice recognition, face/hand geometry, finger imaging. But we have focused today specifically on facial recognition and what it could offer because it is—

Chairman KENNEDY. Let me ask you just to back up. Do you think it is advisable to try and get some international standards so that we are all operating on the same plane, so to speak? Is that advantageous?

Mr. NORTON. Well, that is the direction that the International Civil Aviation Organization is headed, is to look at—they recommended, made a preliminary recommendation that facial recognition be one of the primary biometric technologies. The reason is speed and simplicity. We have passports with photos in them. We issue documents and we are now digitizing those photos and keeping them in records.

By applying a facial recognition template to these stored images, you can very quickly validate who somebody is through automated means. You don't have to have an officer standing there comparing a document to a stored image. The system does it automatically when you use a facial recognition template.

All of our documents have photos. It is the quickest way to get to where we need to be.

Chairman KENNEDY. Well, let me ask you, what is involved in this? You know, if we are to move in that direction now, what generally is the—what do you think is the cost, public-private time frame? What is your own ballpark estimate?

Mr. NORTON. Well, we have been consulting with the officials who do manage the Interagency Border Inspection System on a number of initiatives involving this sort of effort and how the airlines, in fact, might even figure into this of being sort of a second line of defense after the consulates. And really what is required is to take this information that is already available and pull it together, a fairly simple administrative exercise. Apply facial recognition templates, which is a very reasonable cost to do, just simply digitize these images and make them referenceable by facial recognition technology.

I think the biggest challenge is to make this system real-time, to invest in the telecommunications infrastructure to make it a reliable two-way system that can be instantly accessed anywhere around the world. That will be the challenge. I think that our agencies are up to that challenge and already looking into those costs.

Chairman KENNEDY. How far along are we in terms of the technology in this? It is a constantly evolving technology. I am familiar with some of it in my own State of Massachusetts, which has done some of this and is working with the military, primarily, in security areas. But what is your sense? How far along are we in terms of the technology and what is your own assessment on this?

Mr. NORTON. Biometrics have been under development for nearly 20 years, and the U.S. Government was an early adopter of the technologies. They used them to protect very secure national security facilities, nuclear weapons facilities, nuclear power plants. And through the course of this sort of evolution of the technology, they have been made very robust.

Working well and being low cost and easy to implement is another question. But over the past 4 or 5 years, we have also seen the prices drop dramatically, and we have seen the standards put in place that enables these technologies to seamlessly work within a system.

Briefly put, the technologies are robust, they work reliably in many difficult environments, and the standards are in place to move ahead now.

Chairman KENNEDY. How would you compare it to the current I–94 system in terms of integrity and accuracy, speed and improving national security?

Mr. NORTON. Well, the current I–94 system is really a mixed bag. It is very difficult to track somebody out of the country, especially, and it is a laborious process to automate this information.

Proceeding with IBIS along the lines that we discussed—and as Mr. Ziglar recommended—I think is an important first step. The Interagency Border Inspection System has this information already in it that is used to front-load the I–94 system. But it not being taken advantage of. I think now that they have established this link and realized that the Advance Passenger Information program and IBIS and the I–94 program can all operate together is a very important step, and I am glad to see that it is being taken by INS. It will save money and it will help solve the problem of identifying people in the country.

Chairman KENNEDY. You mentioned that the International Air—what is the organization that you mentioned trying to work out a standard process in terms of—

Mr. NORTON. There are actually two. The International Air Transport Association is working on an effort with governments, airports, airlines, and technology providers, and the International Civil Aviation Organization is looking at standardization of travel documents.

Chairman KENNEDY. But they are consistent with their objectives, are they? Is there a consistency with where they are coming out?

Mr. NORTON. Not only a consistency but a synergy. The IATA effort in particular is looking at ways in which biometric information can be voluntarily shared to enable people to move seamlessly through the system, be carefully identified without necessarily being slowed down. People have tended to forget in this debate that we can't slow down commerce and we can't inconvenience the traveler to the point where the industry is disrupted and commerce is disrupted to the United States. We feel these efforts, if carefully coordinated, can make progress in the security area without diminishing commerce, international commerce to the United States.

Chairman KENNEDY. Mr. Papademetriou, let me just ask you your reaction for developing a Northern American perimeter strategy to combat terrorism.

Mr. PAPADEMETRIOU. This is certainly one of the areas that we must explore systematically with our Canadian friends initially, and gradually, as the capabilities of our Mexican friends develop further, with the Mexicans, too.

This is really all about adding an additional bite at the apple in terms of defending ourselves. The outside—the real first line of defense, as we heard earlier, is, of course, the visa issuance process.

I think what Mr. Norton is suggesting, we have recommended the same thing, but a pre-inspection system becomes a second line of defense.

The third one becomes trying to really keep people outside of the perimeter.

Our neighbors, both Canada and Mexico, are assets and they can be made into far greater assets if we work with them rather than being liabilities, which is what some people perhaps might try to do. So, fundamentally, we are going to be building, if we adopt some sort of a perimeter defense or a defense of the North American space, we will be adding an additional and welcome redundancy to protecting ourselves. And it makes sense both in terms of defense but also in terms of protecting and advancing our economic interests.

Chairman KENNEDY. Thank you.

Dr. Butterfield, your view about the national identification system for U.S. citizens and foreign nationals in the U.S.?

Ms. BUTTERFIELD. Well, Mr. Chairman, I think that that is a line that this Nation has not crossed until now, and I would urge us to approach the question with a lot of cautions and concerns about civil liberties, and with the question that my colleague asked earlier about would it really do anything to make us safer and more secure. If I were to have to carry a national I.D. card and everyone else did and every immigrant coming in had some kind of card, then the question is, again, what does that tell us? Do I have to show it every time I buy groceries, every time I make a bank transaction, every time I rent an apartment?

What would its use be? What would a valid use be? What would an overreaching use be? I think those are all questions I would want to see considered before taking that step forward.

Chairman KENNEDY. What about foreign nationals?

Ms. BUTTERFIELD. Well, again, I think that the perimeter strategy, the layers of security and defense are the most effective ones. I think, again, we have a problem with interior verification. How do INS officials or employers, for that matter, know to ask, you know, me for my I.D. or not, because I am a U.S. citizen, but yet ask an immigrant to show some kind of authorization. And I venture to say that Mr. Papademetriou would be asked more often than Ms. Butterfield would. And so then we get into issues about profiling and discrimination.

Chairman KENNEDY. Maybe not in Boston.

[Laughter.]

Senator KENNEDY. Senator DeWine?

Senator DEWINE. Mr. Chairman, thank you. Let me first thank you, Mr. Chairman, for holding this hearing. It is a very important hearing, and I appreciate you doing it very much.

I have, Mr. Chairman, a statement which I would ask just to be made a part of the record.

[The prepared statement of Senator DeWine follows:]

STATEMENT OF HON. MIKE DEWINE, A U.S. SENATOR FROM THE STATE OF OHIO

Chairman Kennedy, thank you for agreeing to hold this important hearing on our efforts to deter terrorism through immigration controls. I thank our witnesses for coming to testify today, as well.

Before I say anything else, I want to make it perfectly clear that I am not here to discourage legal immigration into our country. We are—and always have been—a nation of immigrants. However, following the tragic events of September 11th, we awoke to a whole new world. We now are rethinking many of our nation's policies—from national security measures and intelligence gathering to domestic law enforcement and public health emergency procedures. Our immigration policies are also at the a significant part of the debate on anti-terrorism controls.

In examining current immigration policy and the terrorist threat, we are presented with many questions: Do we focus on trying to keep track of aliens we allow into the United States? Or, do we focus our limited resources on screening those who have asked permission to enter our country? The reality is that we must do both. We must do a better job of screening aliens who enter the country, while at the same time keep track of when and where those aliens enter and exit, and where they are while they are here.

Let me talk for a moment about the scope of what we're facing. Last year, the INS performed 529.6 million inspections of individuals who crossed our borders either by land, sea, or air. As Commissioner Ziglar noted in congressional testimony last week, over a half-billion personal contacts were made with INS inspectors at our ports-of-entry. After deducting American citizens who were inspected, 352 million aliens were inspected in 2000. A little less than a third of those aliens are permanent residents. That leaves 255 million inspections of temporary "nonimmigrant" aliens who are crossing at U.S. ports-of-entry.

It appears that this is the pool of entries in which we are searching to find terrorists and others who are coming into the United States for illicit purposes. Out of 255 million inspections, how on earth are our law enforcement and other agencies responsible for these individuals' entry supposed to identify 19 terrorists?

That's certainly a vast and overwhelming challenge. But, at the same time, it is a challenge that we must meet. Congress expects it. The American people expect it. Today, we want to know what needs to be done meet this daunting task.

While I believe we can meet the challenges we face, I also believe that it can be done only with the help of technology. I would like to hear our panelists' ideas about how technology can be used to lessen the terrorist threat with regard to immigration controls and technology. What is your plan for using all available technology to address immigration concerns?

Let me tell you what I have been thinking. In the Senate's recently passed anti-terrorism package, I asked the Attorney General, in consultation with appropriate agencies, to report to Congress on how we can use our national biometric systems, such as the FBI's Integrated Automated Fingerprint Identification System (IAFIS), to better identify potential terrorists. Specifically, I asked how we can use the automated fingerprint system to identify a person who holds a foreign passport or a visa and may be wanted in connection with a criminal or intelligence investigation in the United States or abroad. The idea is that we would use the automated system to gather this information before the issuance of a visa or entry into—or exit out of—the United States.

I recognize that current INS technology is outdated and insufficient to meet the new demands. We should leverage the substantial investment taxpayers have made in the IAFIS system to create a system of identification and verification that is fully integrated with all relevant federal, state, and local agencies—all in real-time. Currently, IAFIS has more than 48 million images and exchanges information with almost all federal, state, and local law enforcement agencies. I am not saying that this system is perfect, but I am saying that we should use all of our available resources at our disposal.

Again, thank you for participating today. I am looking forward to hearing from our witnesses.

Senator DEWINE. Mr. Norton, I am very interested in the use of biometric technology to enhance security at our borders. I think we are going to have to find a way to quickly implement this type of technology. Over the last couple weeks, I have attended a number of hearings here at the Capitol where biometric technology has been discussed, and discussed at length.

Witnesses have testified regarding the prospects for biometric technology and have given examples of where that technology is already in use. It has really, though, become clear to me that there are two distinct uses for biometric technology. Biometric technology can be used to verify the identity of an alien who is holding a visa, or biometric technology could be used to establish the identity of an alien who applies for a visa or entry in the United States.

Most of the examples I have heard are applications of biometric technology to verify identity. The State Department cites the new laser visas or border crossing cards which incorporate biometric technology. The biometric technology in these so-called smart cards is really just to verify if the person holding the card is the person to which the visa was originally issued. There is no biometric search done by the State Department when that individual is initially issued that visa.

Now, when the State Department issues the original visa, it relies on the information provided by the individual and the name check process described by Ambassador Ryan. If the individual provides false information to the State Department, biometric verification and a laser visa doesn't really tell us anything very useful.

I think we have a similar situation with the INS INSPASS system, and in that case, the hand scan and the accompanying card merely verify the identity of the card holder.

Now, I understand that the IDENT system could be used, can be used to establish the identity of individuals who have been entered into the system because they have been repeatedly caught entering into the country illegally.

Now, aside from that limited use, are there any biometric systems that are currently in use to establish the identity of aliens who want to enter the United States? And a related question is: If we want to positively establish the identity of aliens entering the United States, don't we really need a biometric system in place at our consular offices overseas? And don't we need a real-time biometric identification system at our ports of entry for aliens who have not gone through the normal visa application process?

A long question and I apologize, but I am sure you can handle it.

Mr. NORTON. You raised a number of issues. First of all, you are right. Verification is great technology once you know who somebody is and you can verify who they are, link them to an identity and a document. From that point forward, verification operates very smoothly and effectively. INSPASS has done so in complete security for 8 years, and other countries have had similar success.

But you do have to make sure that you know who you are dealing with, and that is why the criteria so far have been strict as to who is enrolled in the INSPASS system. But how do we bridge that and actually move into visa issuance and know who we are dealing with?

There are a number of technologies that can be used. You can streamline the interface between IDENT and the FBI IAFIS system to do criminal record checks during the application process for a visa. It will require some investment to do that, but it would enable finger images to be checked against the law enforcement database held by the FBI.

Another technology—

Senator DEWINE. Excuse me. How big a deal is that as far as a cost? Do you have any idea?

Mr. NORTON. Well, I think the Department of Justice is looking into that now, and investment is fairly significant. It is about several hundred million dollars, I believe, to bring it into—

Senator DEWINE. But clearly doable.

Mr. NORTON. But it is clearly doable.

Senator DEWINE. Yes.

Mr. NORTON. The second technology that can be used, another very highly accurate technology, is iris recognition, but there is no database of iris recognition enrollees. So once you have identified somebody that way or start a record with iris recognition, it is very effective at identifying a person at a later stage in a one-to-many sort of search.

The third technology that can be used and the one that we spoke to earlier was facial recognition. It may not be able to automate that process, but it can be used very effectively to call up a list of possibilities. If a consular official who acquires a digital image from an applicant for a visa checks against a database of images with that same image that they are acquiring, they should be able to ascertain whether or not that person may be wanted, may be known to intelligence authorities as a possible terrorist. So it can be used as an effective one-to-many search as long as there is human participation in that determination.

You talked about real-time access to biometric information, and that is precisely what we were recommending, and that is that we take the images that we are currently containing in separate databases, images of U.S. passport holders, of alien resident card holders, border crosser card holders, visa holders, and consolidate that information so that we can make quick, real-time checks, even at the airline counter as people try to board their flight to the United States. It does us no good to know that person is already on the flight and headed here, not only from a legal standpoint but from a terrorist threat. And by making IBIS real-time and enabling those checks using facial recognition, at least initially—because we have that data, we have that information, we can use it to automate the process quickly—we can make real progress.

Senator DEWINE. Well, your testimony has been very helpful, and I think your answer was very helpful. And I appreciate it very much.

Let me ask Dr. Butterfield a question which maybe is a little—I don't know if it is out of line, but I know that it is in your area. It has to do with one of the U.S. Supreme Court decisions from June of this year relating to the detention of aliens, the Davis case.

My understanding of that case is that in some circumstances the U.S. Government must release aliens who are supposed to be deported. Let me give the example.

Say, for example, we have an alien who has entered the country with forged or false documents. That person has come into the U.S. and at some point we catch him and determine that he is deportable. But we find out that he is a citizen of a country that we don't have diplomatic relations with, Cuba, for example.

My understanding is that the Supreme Court has said that we cannot hold that individual in detention for more than 6 months.

Now, my question is: What happens with these deportable aliens? Do we just let them go in the United States? Or are they put on some form of probation? What actually happens?

Ms. BUTTERFIELD. Mr. DeWine, I think that you are correct to a certain point. The *Zadvydas* decision said basically that we can't just impose life sentences to imprisonment on someone merely because their home country won't take them back.

But I think it really left open the question and said the Government has to weigh and balance. If the person is truly a danger to national security or to the community, then that is a legitimate Government interest that will be balanced with the individual's liberty interest. And so it merely mandated, I think, the Department of Justice to make that determination on an ongoing basis. And it urged them to look at, yes, could conditions of release be imposed that would guarantee safety and security and balance those needs.

I think to date—I was just told this morning, as a matter of fact—that of the some 3,500 people detained in that very situation, only about 300 have been released. But I think the Court tried to strike a balance there.

Senator DEWINE. Thank you.

Thank you, Mr. Chairman.

Chairman KENNEDY. We thank all of you very much. We will be keeping in touch with you. It was very, very interesting testimony, and we are very grateful for it.

The Committee stands in recess.

[Whereupon, at 12:45 p.m., the Subcommittee was adjourned.]

[A submission for the record follows.]

SUBMISSION FOR THE RECORD

Statement of Hon. Charles E. Grassley, a U.S. Senator from the State of Iowa

Thank you, Mr. Chairman.

This hearing is simply one of many that our Committee will have in order to focus on ways to deter terrorism. Terrorists are taking advantage of our immigration system. They roam freely within our borders under the radar screen of the INS, the State Department, and other law enforcement agencies. There is unanimous agreement that we must secure our borders, and more closely monitor those we have let in.

First, federal agencies need to better share information. The INS needs all relevant information at its disposal to identify and track down immigrants who are on the "watch lists" of other agencies.

Second, we should implement the technologies needed to prevent illegal or criminal aliens from entering. We need to create tamper-resistant visas and passports. We need to invest in an effective biometric system, and provide the scanners to read the information on border crossing cards. Mr. Ziglar lays out a number of technology initiatives in his testimony, and has instructed his staff to expedite database improvements. He specifically mentions the Student Exchange Visitor Information System.

Unfortunately, delay in the implementation of this system has and may continue to have detrimental effects on our nation's security. I find this delay unacceptable. We want to help the colleges and universities, and in turn, I believe that the colleges and universities will want to help us in our war on terrorism.

Last week, I wrote Attorney General John Ashcroft and requested immediate consideration of federal funding to speed up implementation of the student tracking system. I propose that the Department of Justice use a portion of the emergency antiterrorism funds approved by Congress to fund the start-up of the student tracking system. Additionally, the Department should clearly outline the responsibilities of schools who wish to retain foreign students.

Finally, I realize that the INS does not have the enforcement tools to go after every foreign student whose visa expires. And, even if Federal agencies are sharing data and using the best technology we can create, the INS will still face problems in "catching the bad guys."

These are situations in which we can enlist state and local support. By implementing Section 133 of the Illegal Immigration Reform and Immigrant Responsibility Act, the Department of Justice can enter into agreements with local law enforcement agencies in order to allow qualified officers to help in the investigation, apprehension, or detention of illegal aliens.

The enemy could be among us and the threat certainly remains on our soil. Now is the time to stop talking and start acting. We've already identified a number of problems and concrete solutions. We need to move forward with the proposals that we've discussed since September 11.

I thank the Chair and look forward to the testimony from our witnesses.